OUTDOOR ENTERTAINING

Enjoyment is the theme of this
cookbook, and we admit we enjoyed compiling it.
With it you can plan relaxed and happy family
occasions with creative but often surprisingly
simple recipes. Our party menus range from
well-thought-out brunches and lunches
to a spectacular wedding breakfast.
Look, too, for our special salads and super desserts.

EDITOR
Pamela Clark

PHOTOGRAPHER
Russell Brooks

HOME ECONOMISTS
Barbara Northwood
Agnes Lee
Laura Robertson
Lucy Clayton

FOOD STYLIST
Jacqui Hing

KITCHEN ASSISTANT
Amy Wong

ART DIRECTOR
Robbylee Phelan

OUR COVER: Chili Shrimp (p.45)
Tomatoes with Zucchini Filling (p. 35)
Corn with Parmesan Mayonnaise (p. 37)

Cover photography by Brian Leatart; food styling by Karen Gillingham; prop
styling by Kim Wong. "Valencia" pilsners, copper au gratin courtesy of
Williams-Sonoma; red bowl by Waechtersbach; spoon by Patino-Wolf.

©1988, California Magazines, Inc.
Printed by Dai Nippon Ltd, Tokyo, Japan
Published by California Magazines, Inc.,
11601 Wilshire Blvd., Los Angeles, CA, and
Australian Consolidated Press,
54-58 Park Street, Sydney, NSW Australia

ISBN 0-945729-02-2

CONTENTS

BARBECUES 4

Your outdoor entertaining can be just as venturesome and varied as your lunch or dinner parties. Here is a host of new and imaginative recipes for meats and seafood, plus eight pages of salads. Don't overlook tantalizing sauces, mustards and savory butters.

BRUNCHES 46

A relaxed and chatty brunch is one of the most pleasant ways to entertain. To make your brunch go smoothly, we have provided some dishes that can be prepared ahead. Others need to be cooked a moment or two before they are eaten.

LUNCHES 66

We have devised three lunch menus: chicken and champagne for celebrations, vegetarian for a change of taste and pace, and a clever and appealing dieters' meal.

DESSERTS 77

These are the grand finale to your entertaining—seven pages of delightful desserts for every taste, occasion and season.

PICNICS 84

A picnic is one of the most pleasant ways to spend a day. We offer a charming menu for two, and a more robust one for a family of six.

WEDDING BREAKFAST 92

These days many people do their own Wedding Breakfast at home. Our splendid menu is for 50 people, but we show you how to vary quantities. A luscious Croquembouche serves as wedding cake.

CELEBRATION 102

This menu is planned for an at-home young people's celebration, such as a twenty-first birthday or an engagement party. We have given pointers on how to prepare for more than the 25 guests the menu serves. There's a special cake to end the meal.

GARDEN PARTY 108

Choose a warm evening to have a garden party. Food should be delicate and eye-catching. We offer eleven savory recipes and three sweet treats.

SAUSAGE SIZZLE 116

This children's party menu offers good, nourishing food without sacrificing taste and attractiveness, plus Kim the Caterpillar, an easy-to-do party cake.

DRINKS 122

Add sparkle to your parties with original drinks. Here are six clever ways to make champagne go further and look prettier, four punches (some with alcohol, some without) that are popular and inexpensive, and three clever ideas to make coffee special.

INDEX 127

Credits

We are pleased to acknowledge generous help from Mikasa, Orrefors, Villeroy and Boch, and Wedgwood.

Your barbecue, at home or on holidays, at any season of the year, and for just the family or for expected or unexpected guests, can be as attractive and varied as your lunch or dinner parties. Here is a host of new and imaginative recipes with sections on Beef, Pork, Lamb, Chicken (with game birds such as Quail), and Seafoods, including Lobster, Shrimp, Trout and Snapper. There are also eight pages of wonderful salads and some clever ways to prepare vegetables to add color—and food value—to your barbecues. And don't overlook the tantalizing sauces, mustards and savory butters. The wide variety of barbecues in use today means we cannot give suggested cooking times. Barbecuing is usually done in your own backyard, or now that inner-city living is becoming more popular, it can be done on the smallest of patios using one of the portable-type barbecues. A marinade tenderizes and increases the flavor of the food. In most cases we have suggested several hours or overnight. Overnight is best, but time does not always permit this. A few recipes specify only an hour or so—this is for a more delicate flavor. Here are some practical points:

• Always start your barbecue at least 1½ hours before cooking.
• The smoky flavor from barbecued food is the big attraction—the most important rule is to cook over hot coals, not flames.
• Many barbecues have a solid plate and an open rack. Foods that drip or are basted while cooking are usually best cooked on the rack.
• Use long-handled tongs, forks and brushes for basters and butters. An old pan or two is useful for doing last-minute sauces and so on, rather than rushing back into the kitchen.
• When using wooden skewers for barbecuing, it is essential to soak them to minimize burning. They are best soaked overnight.

A Family Barbecue

Select from the meaty recipes to suit your family's tastes. The old favorites—Bean Salad and Coleslaw—are here in an updated version.

CRUNCHY COLESLAW
1 cup cooked brown rice
¼ curly leaf cabbage, shredded
2 sticks celery, sliced
1 red apple, quartered, sliced
1 carrot, grated
¼ cup seedless raisins
DRESSING
½ cup mayonnaise
¼ cup light sour cream
1 teaspoon French mustard
black pepper

Combine rice, cabbage, celery, apple, carrot and raisins in salad bowl, pour Dressing over, toss lightly.

Dressing: Combine all ingredients in screw-top jar, shake well.

   Serves 6.

SIRLOIN STEAK PARCELS
6 sirloin steaks
1 tablespoon soy sauce
1 clove garlic, crushed
2 x ¾-oz packages French onion
    soup mix
1 large onion, sliced
1 cup dry red wine

Rub steaks with combined soy sauce and garlic, stand for several hours or refrigerate overnight. Place each steak on a sheet of aluminum foil large enough to enclose it completely. Sprinkle 2 teaspoons soup mix, a few onion slices and 2 tablespoons red wine over each steak. Seal steaks tightly in foil, barbecue until cooked as desired. It is not necessary to turn steaks.

    Serves 6.

RUM AND ORANGE FRUIT KEBABS
1 pineapple
8 oz strawberries
3 kiwifruit, quartered
3 bananas, quartered
RUM ORANGE BASTE
1 teaspoon grated orange rind
½ cup orange juice
2 teaspoons lemon juice
¼ cup honey
2 tablespoons rum
pinch ground cinnamon

Peel and core pineapple, cut into chunks. Skewer all fruit onto large skewers. Brush with Rum Orange Baste. Barbecue, turning and brushing frequently with Rum Orange Baste. Serve hot.
Rum Orange Baste: Combine all ingredients well.

    Makes about 12 kebabs.

SAUSAGES WITH PRUNES AND BACON
12 thick link sausages
8 oz pitted prunes
6 bacon slices

Prick sausages with a skewer, place sausages in pan, cover with hot water, bring to boil, simmer 10 minutes uncovered, drain, cool. Cut a slit in the side of each sausage, place 3 prunes in each, wrap in half a bacon slice, secure with toothpick. Barbecue until cooked.

    Serves 6.

LEMON-MARINATED LAMB CHOPS
6 lamb loin chops
1 onion, peeled
1 clove garlic, crushed
1 bay leaf
2 teaspoons dried oregano leaves
½ cup olive oil
2 tablespoons lemon juice

Place chops in dish in single layer. Process or blend onion, garlic, bay leaf and oregano with oil and lemon juice. Pour marinade over chops, cover, marinate several hours or refrigerate overnight. Barbecue until tender; baste with marinade often during cooking.

    Serves 6.

ZUCCHINI BURGERS
1 lb ground beef
1 small onion, grated
3 small (6 oz) zucchini, grated
1 teaspoon soy sauce
1 teaspoon grated fresh ginger
1 egg yolk
6 hamburger buns
1 tomato, sliced
1 onion, sliced, extra
lettuce

Combine beef, onion, zucchini, soy sauce, ginger and egg yolk. Shape into 6 patties. Barbecue on lightly oiled plate until done. Serve on toasted, buttered buns with tomato, extra onion and lettuce.

Makes 6 burgers.

CHICKEN WITH BEER TOMATO BASTE
6 large chicken pieces
2 chicken stock cubes
10-oz can Tomato Supreme
1 cup beer
¼ cup white vinegar
1 tablespoon Worcestershire sauce
1 teaspoon paprika
1 tablespoon tomato paste
1 tablespoon golden brown sugar

Place chicken in pan, add crumbled stock cubes, cover with hot water, bring to boil, reduce heat, simmer uncovered 15 minutes; drain. Combine Tomato Supreme, beer, vinegar, Worcestershire sauce, paprika, tomato paste and brown sugar in bowl, add chicken. Marinate several hours or overnight, turning occasionally. Barbecue chicken, brushing often with marinade, until golden brown.

Serves 6.

THREE BEAN SALAD WITH SWEET DRESSING
8 oz frozen green beans
8 oz frozen yellow beans
14-oz can red kidney beans, drained
1 small red bell pepper, sliced
1 small onion, sliced
SWEET DRESSING
½ cup oil
3 tablespoons white vinegar
2 tablespoons golden brown sugar
½ teaspoon dry mustard
1 small clove garlic, crushed
1 teaspoon dried basil leaves

Combine thawed beans, rinsed kidney beans, pepper and onion in bowl. Add Dressing, cover, refrigerate several hours or overnight before serving.

SWEET DRESSING: Combine all ingredients in screw-top jar, shake well.

Serves 6.

Beef

Steak is traditionally the most popular of all meats to barbecue; the heat of the barbecue is all-important so that the steaks will be cooked to suit your guests' individual tastes. Mix and match the different cuts of steaks with the various marinades given in this section. A quick but effective tip for barbecuing steaks that have not been marinated is to pour a little beer onto each side of the meat as it is cooking.

RED WINE AND CHILI STEAKS
6 rump steaks
14 oz can beef consommé
1 stick celery, chopped
2 small onions, chopped
1 cup dry red wine
2 tablespoons tomato paste
2 teaspoons Worcestershire sauce
1 teaspoon chili sauce
Combine consommé, celery, onion, wine, tomato paste, Worcestershire sauce and chili sauce in pan, bring to boil, reduce heat, simmer uncovered 20 minutes, cool. Puree mixture in blender or processor, strain, pour over steaks. Marinate several hours or refrigerate overnight. Drain steak, reserve marinade. Barbecue steaks until well browned. Serve with the hot reserved marinade as a sauce.
Serves 6.

TERIYAKI STEAKS
6 pieces rib-eye steak
⅓ cup soy sauce
¼ cup dry red wine
2 cloves garlic, crushed
2 teaspoons grated fresh ginger
2 tablespoons golden brown sugar
1 tablespoon barbecue sauce
Marinate steaks in soy sauce, wine, garlic, brown sugar and barbecue sauce several hours or refrigerate, covered, overnight. Drain steaks, barbecue on both sides until cooked through.
Serves 6.

CRUSTY PEPPER FILLET
3-lb rib-eye roast
2 tablespoons whole black
    peppercorns
1 tablespoon cardamom seeds
1 cup rock salt
3 tablespoons mustard
2 tablespoons oil
1 clove garlic, crushed
2 tablespoons oil, extra
Blend peppercorns and cardamom seeds until coarsely cracked, add salt, blend until lightly crushed. Trim roast, roll, tie in shape with string. Combine mustard, oil and garlic, rub over surface of roast. Roll in peppercorn mixture. Heat extra oil on barbecue plate, brown all sides of roast, continue barbecuing until done as desired, turning frequently. Break off crust before serving.
Serves 6 to 8.

HONEY-GLAZED BEEF SPARERIBS
4 lb beef spareribs
⅓ cup ketchup
⅓ cup honey
1 tablespoon Worcestershire sauce
2 teaspoons soy sauce
1 tablespoon white vinegar
Trim spareribs, combine with ketchup, honey, Worcestershire sauce, soy sauce and vinegar, mix well, stand several hours or refrigerate overnight. Barbecue until tender and golden brown.
Serves 6.

SPINACH BURGERS

1½ lb ground beef
2 tablespoons fruit chutney
1 tablespoon tomato paste
2 teaspoons French mustard
1 clove garlic, crushed
1 egg
SPINACH FILLING
½ x 8 oz package frozen spinach
1 small onion, finely chopped
2 tablespoons grated Parmesan
    cheese
¾ cup stale bread crumbs
pinch ground nutmeg

Combine steak with chutney, tomato paste, mustard, garlic and half the beaten egg in bowl, mix well. Shape into 12 patties. Divide Spinach Filling over 6 patties, leaving a 1-inch edge. Top with remaining 6 patties, press to seal edges. Barbecue until cooked through.

Spinach Filling: Thaw spinach, drain well, mix with onion, cheese, bread crumbs, nutmeg and remaining egg.

BARBECUED GROUND BEEF PIZZA

Use the leanest beef available.

1 lb ground beef
3 bacon slices, chopped
1 large onion, finely chopped
½ teaspoon paprika
½ teaspoon dried oregano leaves
1 clove garlic, crushed
3 tablespoons tomato paste
8 oz mozzarella cheese slices
3 oz mushrooms, sliced
1 small green bell pepper, sliced
1 tomato, sliced
2 tablespoons grated Parmesan
    cheese
½ teaspoon dried basil leaves

Fry bacon until crisp; drain. Combine beef, onion, paprika, oregano and garlic. Press mixture evenly into 11-inch pizza pan. Spread evenly with tomato paste, then cheese, bacon, mushroom, pepper and tomato. Sprinkle with Parmesan cheese and basil. Cover with aluminum foil, barbecue 10 minutes, uncover, drain off juices, barbecue until beef is cooked through, and cheese melted. Drain off juices, serve immediately.

BEER-BASTED SIRLOIN STEAKS
6 sirloin steaks
¼ cup golden brown sugar
1½ tablespoons seeded mustard
1 tablespoon white vinegar
1 cup beer
1 onion, finely chopped
1 bay leaf
Place sugar, mustard, vinegar, beer, onion and bay leaf in pan, bring to boil, reduce heat, simmer gently uncovered 10 minutes, cool. Pour mixture over steaks, stand 1 to 2 hours, turning steaks occasionally. Barbecue until golden brown on both sides.
Serves 6.

SATAY BEEF
1½-lb rump steak
1½ tablespoons soy sauce
2 teaspoons cornstarch
2 tablespoons golden brown sugar
1 teaspoon grated fresh ginger
1 tablespoon water
SATAY SAUCE
¾ cup roasted unsalted peanuts
1 oz butter
1 onion, finely chopped
2 cloves garlic, crushed
1½ teaspoons curry powder
2 teaspoons soy sauce
1 red chile, finely chopped
1¼ cups water
Cut meat into 1-inch pieces. Combine soy sauce, cornstarch, sugar, ginger and water in bowl, add meat, mix well, stand 1 hour. Thread meat onto skewers. Brush meat with oil, barbecue until well browned all over. Serve with Satay Sauce.
Satay Sauce: Blend or process peanuts finely. Melt butter in pan, add onion and garlic, cook 1 minute. Add curry powder and peanuts, stir 1 minute, add soy sauce, chile and water, bring to boil, reduce heat. Simmer Sauce uncovered for 10 minutes or until thick.
Serves 6.

STEAKS IN RED WINE MARINADE
6 T-bone steaks
¾ cup dry red wine
¼ cup oil
¼ cup water
2 tablespoons soy sauce
1 tablespoon golden brown sugar
1 clove garlic, crushed
½ teaspoon ground ginger
½ teaspoon dried oregano leaves
Place steaks in single layer in dish. Combine red wine with remaining ingredients, mix well, pour over steaks, cover, marinate 2 hours or refrigerate overnight, turn steaks occasionally. Barbecue until cooked as desired.
Serves 6.

13

Salads

Select from these salads to serve at your barbecues, parties, lunches or just as part of a meal. All the recipes serve six people. As the number of guests increases, introduce several salads for them to choose from; in this case the servings from these recipes would be enough for about ten people. The amount of Dressing required doesn't always double when the rest of the recipe doubles. For example, as a guide, if you were making four times any one of these recipes you would only need twice the amount of Dressing.

CREAMY APPLE PECAN SALAD
2 Granny Smith apples
2 red Delicious apples
2 tablespoons lemon juice
1½ cups thinly sliced celery
½ cup pecans
DRESSING
½ cup mayonnaise
½ cup sour cream
2 teaspoons lemon juice
1 teaspoon honey
pinch each ground cinnamon and
    ground nutmeg

Core and quarter apples, slice thinly, dip in lemon juice; combine with celery in bowl. Add pecans, toss lightly, serve topped with Dressing.
Dressing: Combine all ingredients.
    Serves 6.

CELERY AND MUSHROOM SALAD
1 lb baloy mushrooms
3 sticks celery, thinly sliced
6 scallions, chopped
1 radicchio lettuce
DRESSING
⅓ cup oil
2 tablespoons white vinegar
½ cup bottled pimientos, sliced

Combine mushrooms, celery and scallions. Spoon over radicchio. Pour Dressing over salad.
Dressing: Combine all ingredients.
    Serves 6.

SPINACH AND OYSTER SALAD
Croutons can be cooked, cooled and stored in an airtight container for a week.

1 bunch silverbeet (about 20 leaves)
18 oysters
CROUTONS
4 slices white bread
1 oz butter
1 tablespoon olive oil
1 clove garlic, crushed
1 tablespoon grated Parmesan
    cheese
1 teaspoon paprika
DRESSING
½ cup oil
1 egg
¼ cup lemon juice
1 tablespoon French mustard
2 tablespoons chopped parsley
1 tablespoon grated Parmesan
    cheese
1 teaspoon Worcestershire sauce
dash Tabasco

Tear spinach leaves into pieces, place in bowl with oysters, toss in enough Dressing just to coat leaves, top with croutons.
Croutons: Trim crusts from bread, cut bread into ½-inch cubes. Melt butter in pan, add oil and garlic, heat until garlic begins to brown. Add bread cubes to pan, coat with butter mixture. place bread cubes on oven tray, bake in moderately hot oven 5 to 10 minutes or until brown. Toss in combined Parmesan cheese and paprika while still warm; cool.
Dressing: Blend or process all ingredients until smooth and thick.
    Serves 6.

TOMATO, OLIVE AND FETA SALAD
1 lb cherry tomatoes
4 oz black olives
12 oz feta cheese, diced
DRESSING
⅓ cup olive oil
2 tablespoons white vinegar
1 clove garlic, crushed
¼ teaspoon dried oregano leaves
¼ teaspoon dried basil leaves

Combine tomatoes, olives and cheese in bowl. Pour over Dressing, stand 1 hour before serving.
Dressing: Combine all ingredients.
    Serves 6.

PEPPER AND PINEAPPLE SALAD
1 medium pineapple
2 kiwifruit
2 red bell peppers
DRESSING
¼ cup oil
2 tablespoons lemon juice
¼ cup chopped parsley
¼ cup chopped fresh mint

Peel pineapple, cut into 1-inch slices, cut each slice into wedges. Peel and slice kiwifruit. Cut peppers into strips. Combine pineapple, kiwifruit and peppers, pour over Dressing and refrigerate 1 hour before serving.
Dressing: Combine all ingredients, strain.
    Serves 6.

CAULIFLOWER, SUGAR PEA AND SHRIMP SALAD
Sugar or snow peas need topping and tailing.

1 small cauliflower
8 oz sugar or snow peas
3 lb small cooked shrimp, shelled
CURRY MAYONNAISE
½ cup mayonnaise
2 teaspoons curry powder
¼ teaspoon Worcestershire sauce
tiny pinch saffron powder

Break cauliflower into flowerets, top and tail sugar peas. Drop cauliflower and sugar peas into pan of boiling water for 1 minute, drain, rinse under cold water until completely cold; drain. Toss in salad bowl with shrimp. Pour Curry Mayonnaise over salad, toss well.
Curry Mayonnaise: Combine all ingredients in bowl, beat together well.
    Serves 6.

Left to right: top, Pepper and Pineapple; Creamy Apple Pecan; center, Tomato, Olive and Feta; Cauliflower, Sugar Pea and Shrimp; bottom, Celery and Mushroom; Spinach and Oyster.

AVOCADO, MANGO AND WALNUT SALAD

2 avocados, peeled, sliced
2 mangoes, peeled, sliced
½ cup walnut pieces
3 bacon slices, finely chopped
1 lettuce
DRESSING
¼ cup olive oil
2 tablespoons lemon juice
1 teaspoon French mustard
1 tablespoon cream

Cook bacon in pan until crisp; drain. Arrange avocado, mango, walnut and bacon over bed of lettuce, top with Dressing.

Dressing: Combine all ingredients in screw-top jar, shake well.

Serves 6.

NEW POTATO SALAD WITH BASIL DRESSING

If preferred, use mint instead of basil.

1 lb small white potatoes
2 tablespoons pine nuts
1 cucumber, sliced
2 teaspoons chopped fresh basil
BASIL DRESSING
1 cup basil leaves, loosely packed
2 cloves garlic, crushed
2 tablespoons pine nuts, toasted
2 tablespoons grated Parmesan
  cheese
½ cup mayonnaise
¼ cup light sour cream

Boil or steam potatoes until tender; drain, place in salad bowl. Place pine nuts (those for Dressing as well) on oven tray, toast in moderate oven 5 to 8 minutes, add the 2 tablespoons pine nuts to potatoes with cucumber, pour Dressing over, toss lightly. Sprinkle with basil.

Basil Dressing: Combine basil, garlic, toasted pine nuts and Parmesan cheese in processor, process until smooth, add mayonnaise and sour cream, process until smooth.

Serves 6.

GOAT CHEESE SALAD WITH MUSTARD DRESSING

Radicchio or red leaf looks pretty with butter lettuce.

1 butter lettuce
1 radicchio lettuce
1 small bunch watercress
1 small bunch curly endive
½ lb fresh goat cheese, sliced thinly
MUSTARD DRESSING
3 tablespoons olive oil
1 tablespoon white vinegar
2 teaspoons French mustard
½ teaspoon dried basil leaves

Arrange salad greens on serving plate, top with cheese, cover, refrigerate until ready to serve. Pour Dressing over just before serving.

Dressing: Combine all ingredients.

Serves 6.

BEET SALAD WITH GINGER DRESSING

4 medium beets
2 limes
6 oranges
½ cup walnut pieces
2 shallots, chopped
3 teaspoons honey
¼ cup oil
1 teaspoon grated fresh ginger

Boil or steam whole beets until tender, about 30 minutes; cool, remove skins. Cut beets into fine strips.

Peel 1 orange and 1 lime finely with vegetable peeler, cut rind into fine strips. Drop rind into pan of boiling water, drain.

Peel oranges thickly and cut into segments; save about ¼ cup orange juice for dressing. Arrange orange segments and beet strips on plate, top with walnuts, shallots and rind. Make dressing by squeezing juice from limes; make up to ½ cup juice with reserved orange juice, add honey and oil. Extract juice from ginger by pressing between 2 teaspoons; add juice to dressing; mix well, pour over salad.

Serves 6.

JULIENNE OF VEGETABLE SALAD
2 red bell peppers
2 green bell peppers
3 sticks celery
2 carrots, peeled
1 cup alfalfa sprouts
DRESSING
½ cup French dressing
3 teaspoons seeded mustard

Cut peppers, celery and carrots into thin strips about 2 inches long, toss in salad bowl with sprouts. Toss lightly with Dressing just before serving.

Dressing: Gradually stir French dressing into mustard.

Serves 6.

WATERCRESS AND RADISH SALAD
6 spinach leaves
3 cups loosely packed watercress
    sprigs
8 radishes, sliced
DRESSING
2 tablespoons oil
1 teaspoon brown sugar
1 teaspoon dry mustard
¼ teaspoon cinnamon
2 tablespoons brown vinegar

Tear spinach into pieces, place in bowl, mix with watercress and radishes, toss lightly with Dressing just before serving.

Dressing: Combine all ingredients in screw-top jar, shake well.

Serves 6.

PECAN AND PASTA SALAD
12 oz large pasta (spiral or
    shell-shaped)
1 red bell pepper, chopped
2 spinach leaves, shredded
⅔ cup pecans
DRESSING
¼ cup oil
⅓ cup white vinegar
1 tablespoon sugar
tiny pinch saffron powder
1 clove garlic, crushed
¼ teaspoon ground coriander
¼ teaspoon ground cardamom

Add pasta gradually to large pan of boiling water, boil uncovered 10 to 15 minutes or until just tender; drain, cool.

Combine pasta with remaining ingredients in salad bowl; toss lightly with Dressing just before serving.

Dressing: Combine all ingredients in screw-top jar, shake well.

Serves 6.

LIMA BEAN SALAD WITH ANCHOVY DRESSING

2 lb frozen or fresh lima beans
5 small tomatoes
5 hard-boiled eggs
18 black olives
ANCHOVY DRESSING
½ x 1½-oz can rolled fillets of anchovies
¼ cup olive oil
2 tablespoons lemon juice
1 clove garlic, crushed

Drop beans into pan of boiling water, boil 3 minutes, drain, rinse under cold water. Peel skins from beans. Quarter tomatoes and eggs. Combine beans, tomatoes, eggs and olives in salad bowl. Pour Anchovy Dressing over, toss lightly.

Anchovy Dressing: Process or blend all ingredients until smooth.

Serves 6.

SPROUT AND SNOW PEA SALAD

1 tablespoon sesame seeds
8 oz snow peas
8 oz broccoli
2 cups bean sprouts
2 shallots, chopped
DRESSING
2 teaspoons grated fresh ginger
¼ cup lemon juice
¼ cup oil
2 teaspoons sugar
pepper

Place sesame seeds in pan, stir constantly over heat until golden brown, remove from hot pan immediately, cool.

Top and tail snow peas, drop into pan of boiling water for 1 minute, drain, rinse under cold water, drain.

Break broccoli into flowerettes, boil or steam for 3 minutes, or until just tender, drain.

Combine snow peas, broccoli, bean sprouts and shallots in salad bowl, toss lightly with Dressing, sprinkle with sesame seeds.

Dressing: Combine all ingredients in screw-top jar, shake well, strain.

Serves 6.

HAM AND BEAN SALAD WITH GREEN PEPPERCORNS

1 lb French green beans
½ lb ham
1 red bell pepper
½ lb cherry tomatoes
DRESSING
½ cup oil
2 tablespoons white vinegar
1 tablespoon green peppercorns,
    drained
1 teaspoon French mustard

Top and tail beans, cut in half lengthwise. Bring pan of water to boil, add beans, cook 3 minutes; drain, rinse under cold water. Cut ham and pepper into thin strips. Combine beans, pepper and tomatoes, pour over Dressing, refrigerate several hours. Before serving, add ham, toss lightly.
Dressing: Combine all ingredients.
    Serves 6.

BROWN RICE AND CABANOSSI SALAD

1 cup brown rice
2 cabanossi (Polish pork sausages),
    sliced
1 red bell pepper, sliced
1 green bell pepper, sliced
4 shallots, chopped
DRESSING
½ cup bottled French dressing
¼ cup sour cream
1 tablespoon chopped fresh dill

Add rice gradually to large pan of boiling water, boil uncovered about 30 minutes or until rice is as tender as desired. Drain, rinse under cold water; drain well.
    Combine rice, cabanossi, peppers and shallots in salad bowl. Pour Dressing over, toss well.
Dressing: Combine all ingredients in screw-top jar, shake well.
    Serves 6.

FRUITY RICE SALAD
¾ cup long-grain rice
½ cup pine nuts
½ cup seedless raisins
1 stick celery, diced
4 shallots, chopped
½ cup walnut pieces
2 tablespoons chopped glacé
    ginger
2 glacé apricots, chopped
DRESSING
¼ cup orange juice
2 tablespoons oil
1 clove garlic, crushed
1 teaspoon grated fresh ginger
2 teaspoons honey
1 teaspoon lemon juice

Add rice gradually to large pan of boiling water, boil uncovered 10 to 15 minutes or until tender, drain; cool. Toast pine nuts in moderate oven 5 to 8 minutes.

Combine all ingredients in salad bowl, toss well with Dressing. Cover, refrigerate several hours before serving.
Dressing: Combine all ingredients in screw-top jar, shake well.
Serves 6.

CONFETTI WILD RICE SALAD

Wild rice is expensive but tastes deliciously different. We've extended ours with white rice. Cook wild rice as directed on package for a crunchy texture, or add it to a pan of boiling water and boil for about 20 minutes or until each grain bursts open.

½ x 6-oz package wild rice
½ cup long-grain white rice
2 shallots, chopped
1 red bell pepper, chopped
DRESSING
¼ cup oil
2 teaspoons lemon juice
1 teaspoon sugar

Cook wild rice as above, add white rice to pan of boiling water, boil rapidly uncovered for 10 minutes or until just tender; drain. Combine wild and white rice with shallots and red bell pepper. Toss well with Dressing. Refrigerate, covered, for several hours before serving.
Dressing: Combine oil, lemon juice and sugar in screw-top jar, shake well.
Serves 6.

COCONUT CREAM RICE RING
1 cup brown rice
2 tablespoons coconut cream
¼ cup chopped roasted hazelnuts
½ cup chopped cucumber
¼ cup chopped mint
2 tablespoons chopped parsley
1 mango, peeled, sliced

Add rice gradually to large pan of boiling water, boil uncovered about 30 minutes or until rice is as tender as desired. Drain, rinse under cold water; drain well.

Combine brown rice with coconut cream, hazelnuts, cucumber, mint and parsley. Pack firmly into lightly oiled ring mold of 3-cup fluid capacity. Cover, refrigerate 30 minutes. Turn rice ring onto plate, decorate with mango.
Serves 6.

Left to right: Brown Rice and Cabanossi Salad; Fruity Rice Salad; Confetti Wild Rice Salad; Coconut Cream Rice Ring.

Pork & Ham

Pork is great for barbecuing. Cook quickly to seal the outside, then barbecue more gently until done as desired. Do not overcook or pork will become dry.

PEPPERED PORK PATTIES
1 lb ground pork
½ cup stale bread crumbs
½ apple, grated
1 small onion, chopped
2 oz (¼ cup) whole black
    peppercorns, coarsely
    crushed

Combine meat, bread crumbs, apple and onion, mix well. Shape mixture into 6 patties, press both sides of patties in peppercorns. Barbecue patties until cooked through.

    Makes 6 patties.

PORK CROQUETTES WITH SPINACH SAUCE
1 lb ground pork
½ oz butter
2 tablespoons cream
1 clove garlic, crushed
8 oz package frozen spinach
1 egg
1½ cups packaged bread crumbs
SPINACH SAUCE
1 onion, chopped
½ oz butter
1 tablespoon all-purpose flour
½ cup chicken stock
⅓ cup cream

Combine pork, soft butter, cream, garlic and half the thawed drained spinach; mix well, refrigerate 30 minutes.

    Shape mixture into 6 sausage shapes with floured hands, dip in beaten egg, then bread crumbs. Barbecue gently on oiled plate, turning constantly until cooked through and golden brown, serve with Spinach Sauce.

Spinach Sauce: Sauté onion in butter, add flour, stir until lightly browned, gradually stir in stock and remaining thawed drained spinach; stir until sauce boils and thickens, add cream.

    Makes 6 croquettes.

CRUMBED SKEWERED SAUSAGES
12 thin pork link sausages
6 slices stale whole-grain bread
¼ cup chopped parsley
¼ grated Parmesan cheese
¼ cup slivered almonds
1 teaspoon dried basil leaves
2 eggs
2 tablespoons mayonnaise
2 tablespoons seeded mustard

Lightly prick sausages, simmer in pan of water for 10 minutes, drain, cool, remove skin. Combine bread, parsley, cheese, almonds and basil in processor, process until finely crumbed. Push wooden skewers through sausages, dip sausages in combined eggs, mayonnaise and mustard, roll in bread crumbs. Barbecue until crumbs are golden brown and sausages cooked.

    Serves 6.

SWEET AND SOUR SPARERIBS

12 pork slices or spareribs
⅓ cup plum sauce
1 tablespoon soy sauce
2 tablespoons brown sugar
1 teaspoon grated fresh ginger
2 tablespoons white vinegar
2 tablespoons tomato sauce
1 tablespoon hoisin sauce
2 shallots, chopped

Combine spareribs with plum sauce, soy sauce, brown sugar, ginger, vinegar, tomato sauce, hoisin sauce and shallots. Stand several hours, or refrigerate overnight; turn spareribs occasionally. Barbecue until tender, brushing occasionally with remaining marinade.

Serves 6.

SATAY PORK

2 lb pork loin chops
1 small onion, grated
1 teaspoon grated fresh ginger
2 cloves garlic, crushed
1 teaspoon ground fennel seeds
1 teaspoon ground coriander
1 teaspoon ground caraway seeds
1 red chili, finely chopped

PINEAPPLE KEBABS

1½ 20-oz cans sliced pineapple
1 cucumber

SATAY SAUCE

¼ cup roasted unsalted peanuts
1 tablespoon oil
1 onion, finely chopped
2 cloves garlic, crushed
1 teaspoon grated fresh ginger
1 teaspoon turmeric
¼ teaspoon ground cardamom
¼ teaspoon ground cumin
½ cup water
½ cup coconut milk

Remove rind and bones from chops, cut meat into thin slices. Combine meat with onion, ginger, garlic, fennel, coriander, caraway and chili; stand 30 minutes. Thread meat onto skewers. Barbecue until tender, brushing occasionally with a little oil. Serve with Satay Sauce and Pineapple Kebabs.

Pineapple Kebabs: Cut each pineapple slice into 6 pieces. Cut unpeeled, seeded cucumber into chunks. Skewer pineapple and cucumber, barbecue lightly.

Satay Sauce: Blend or process peanuts until fine. Heat oil in pan, add onion, garlic and ginger, cook 1 minute. Add turmeric, cardamom, cumin and peanuts, mix well. Add water, bring to boil, reduce heat, simmer uncovered 5 minutes, mix in coconut milk.

Serves 6.

PORK WITH ORANGE MAPLE SAUCE

6 pork chops
1 tablespoon oil
1 onion, finely chopped
2 teaspoons grated orange rind
½ cup orange juice
¼ cup maple syrup
¼ teaspoon ground rosemary
2 teaspoons cornstarch
¼ cup water

Heat oil in pan, add onion, sauté few minutes, stir in orange rind and juice, syrup and rosemary, pour over chops, mix well. Stand several hours or refrigerate overnight. Barbecue chops until tender, place marinade in pan, stir in blended cornstarch and water, stir until mixture boils and thickens. Serve over chops, topped with thick orange slices.

Serves 6.

BUTTERFLY STEAKS WITH MUSTARD SAUCE

6 pork butterfly steaks
flour, pepper, paprika
1 oz butter, melted
1 tablespoon oil
MUSTARD SAUCE
1 cup chicken stock
2 tablespoons brandy
2 tablespoons cream
2 tablespoons seeded mustard
1 teaspoon dried tarragon leaves
2 tablespoon capers
10 oz sour cream
2 tablespoons chopped chives

Toss steaks in flour seasoned with pepper and paprika. Barbecue until tender, brushing often with combined butter and oil. Serve with Mustard Sauce.

Mustard Sauce: Combine stock, brandy, cream, mustard and tarragon in pan. Boil uncovered 5 minutes, or until liquid has reduced by half; stir in capers, sour cream and chives, reheat without boiling.

Serves 6.

HAM STEAKS WITH APRICOT GLAZE

6 ham steaks
½ cup apricot jam
½ teaspoon cumin
¼ cup French dressing
1 tablespoon dry sherry

Heat jam, cumin, dressing and sherry in pan, pour over ham steaks, marinate several hours, or overnight in refrigerator. Barbecue ham steaks on both sides until heated through.

Serves 6.

HAM STEAKS WITH GLAZED APPLES

6 ham steaks
1 oz butter
2 red apples, quartered, sliced
½ cup brown sugar
2 tablespoons golden syrup
¼ cup lemon juice
1 teaspoon grated lemon rind
½ cup canned apple juice
1 tablespoon brandy

Heat butter in pan, add apple slices, cook quickly until lightly browned, remove from pan. Add sugar, syrup and lemon juice to remaining butter in pan, stir without boiling until sugar is dissolved. Add lemon rind, apple juice and brandy, boil few minutes or until sauce is thick. Barbecue ham steaks until heated through, top with apple slices, then hot sauce.

Serves 6.

GLAZED PORK FILLETS
6 small pork fillets
¼ cup tomato sauce
¼ cup honey
¼ teaspoon five-spice powder
2 teaspoons soy sauce
1 clove garlic, crushed
Combine fillets with tomato sauce, honey, five-spice powder, soy sauce and garlic, stand 1 hour, turning occasionally. Barbecue until tender, brushing occasionally with remaining marinade.
    Serves 6.

Mustards and Sauces

The sauces are meant to be made and used within a short time. The mustards, however, will keep for about a month; refrigerate after opening.

SWEET AND SOUR APRICOT SAUCE
⅓ cup dried apricots
1½ cups water
1 shallot, chopped
½ cup white vinegar
⅓ cup honey
¼ cup tomato sauce
3 tablespoons oil
½ teaspoon soy sauce
Combine apricots and water in pan, bring to boil, reduce heat, simmer 15 minutes or until tender; drain, reserve ½ cup liquid. Combine apricots and reserved liquid in blender, blend until smooth. Combine apricot puree and remaining ingredients in pan, bring to boil, reduce heat, simmer 1 minute. Serve hot.
    Makes about 2 cups.

BARBECUE SAUCE
Store any leftover sauce covered and refrigerated.

2 onions, sliced
2 cloves garlic, crushed
2 tablespoons oil
¼ cup red wine vinegar
¼ cup brown sugar
2 tablespoons seeded mustard
1 tablespoon Worcestershire sauce
14 ½ oz can tomatoes
1 teaspoon salt
2 tablespoons tomato paste
Sauté onions and garlic in oil until tender. Stir in vinegar, sugar, mustard, Worcestershire sauce, undrained tomatoes, salt and tomato paste. Bring to boil, reduce heat, simmer uncovered for 30 minutes. Puree Sauce in blender or push through sieve. Serve hot or cold.
    Makes about 2 cups.

HERBED TOMATO SAUCE
2¼ lb ripe tomatoes, chopped
1 onion, chopped
1 clove garlic, crushed
1 carrot, chopped
2 tablespoons oil
1 teaspoon sugar
¼ cup chicken stock
3 teaspoons Worcestershire sauce
½ teaspoon dried basil leaves
½ teaspoon dried oregano leaves
Sauté onion, garlic and carrot in oil 5 minutes. Stir in tomatoes, sugar, stock, Worcestershire sauce and herbs, bring to boil, reduce heat, cover, simmer 30 minutes. Puree mixture in blender or push through sieve. Return mixture to pan, bring to boil, reduce heat, simmer further 15 minutes uncovered. Store for up to a week, covered, in refrigerator.
    Makes 3 cups.

MADEIRA MUSTARD
½ cup (3 oz) white mustard seeds
1 teaspoon salt
½ cup white vinegar
½ cup oil
½ cup madeira
1 tablespoon brandy

Combine mustard seeds and salt in blender, blend 30 seconds. Add vinegar, oil, madeira and brandy, blend until thickened. Spoon into container, cover, stand for 2 days. Store in cool, dark place. Keep refrigerated after opening.

Makes 1½ cups.

FRESH HERB MUSTARD
½ cup (3 oz) white mustard seeds
1 cup ground almonds
1 cup oil
1 cup white vinegar
3 teaspoons salt
¼ cup port
1 tablespoon chopped fresh
    marjoram
1 tablespoon chopped fresh oregano
1 tablespoon chopped fresh thyme.

Combine mustard seeds and almonds in blender, blend 30 seconds. Add oil, vinegar, salt, port and herbs, blend until thickened. Spoon into container, cover, stand for 2 days. Store in cool, dark place. Keep refrigerated after opening.

Makes 2½ cups.

GREEN PEPPERCORN MUSTARD
½ cup (3 oz) white mustard seeds
1 tablespoon whole white
    peppercorns
2 teaspoons salt
½ cup oil
½ cup dry sherry
½ cup white vinegar
1 tablespoon canned green
    peppercorns, drained

Combine mustard seeds, white peppercorns and salt in blender, blend 30 seconds. Add oil, sherry and vinegar, blend until thickened. Stir in green peppercorns. Spoon into container, cover, stand for 2 days. Store in cool, dark place. Keep refrigerated after opening.

Makes 1½ cups.

HOT GRAINY MUSTARD
½ cup (3 oz) white mustard seeds
1 tablespoon whole white
    peppercorns
2 teaspoons whole black
    peppercorns
2 teaspoons salt
½ cup oil
½ cup dry sherry
½ cup white vinegar

Combine mustard seeds, peppercorns and salt in blender, blend 30 seconds. Add oil, sherry and vinegar, blend until thickened. Spoon into container, cover, stand for 2 days. Store in cool, dark place. Keep refrigerated after opening.

Makes 1½ cups.

PARSLEY PARMESAN SAUCE
½ cup walnut pieces
½ cup grated Parmesan cheese
2 cloves garlic, crushed
1 cup olive oil
salt
1 cup chopped parsley
1 tablespoon lemon juice

Combine all ingredients in blender or processor. Blend on high speed until smooth. Store, covered, for up to a week in refrigerator.

Makes 1½ cups.

LEMON CAPER MAYONNAISE
2 egg yolks
1 cup oil
⅓ cup lemon juice
1 tablespoon tarragon vinegar
1 tablespoon capers
1 gherkin

Beat egg yolks in processor or blender until thick, add oil very slowly, beating constantly until thick. Add lemon juice, vinegar, capers and gherkin, blend until smooth.

Makes about 1½ cups.

HORSERADISH CREAM SAUCE
½-pint jar whipping cream
2 tablespoons lemon juice
¼ cup bottled horseradish
½ teaspoon dry mustard

Beat cream until soft peaks form. Stir in combined lemon juice, horseradish and mustard. Refrigerate, covered, until ready to serve.

Makes 1½ cups.

Lamb

If you want to barbecue chops, try serving them with one of our mustards or sauces (see page 26). Or try the racks or boned leg of lamb. The trend is to serve lamb slightly pink so it retains its juiciness. Cook the outside of the lamb quickly, then cook more gently until done to suit individual tastes.

BARBECUED LEG OF LAMB WITH APRICOT BACON ROLLS
1 boned leg of lamb
4 bacon slices
⅓ cup finely chopped dried apricots
2 shallots, finely chopped

Trim lamb of excess fat. Cut bacon slices in half crossways. Soak apricots in boiling water for few minutes, drain, pat dry, mix with shallots. Roll a teaspoonful of apricot mixture in each piece of bacon. Cut 8 deep pockets into underside of lamb, place a bacon roll in each one. Barbecue lamb over gentle heat until tender.

Serves 8.

BARBECUED LAMB KEBABS
1½ lb ground lamb
2 onions, grated
2 tablespoons chopped parsley
2 cloves garlic, crushed
2 tablespoons barbecue sauce
4 oz baby squash
½ lb cherry tomatoes

Combine lamb, onion, parsley, garlic and barbecue sauce, mix well. Shape into balls, thread onto skewers, alternating with squash and cherry tomatoes. Barbecue until browned and cooked through.

Makes about 12 skewers.

RACKS OF LAMB WITH PARSLEY PEPPER CRUST

6 racks lamb, with 4 chops in each
2 oz butter
1 tablespoon mango chutney
2 teaspoons French mustard
1 clove garlic, crushed
2 teaspoons lemon juice
black pepper
1 cup chopped parsley

Trim excess fat from lamb. Combine softened butter, chutney, mustard, garlic and lemon juice in bowl. Spread over back of each lamb rack, then sprinkle thickly with coarsely ground pepper and parsley. Press mixture on gently with hand. Barbecue until meat is tender; do not turn racks.

Serves 6.

FRESH HERB LAMB CHOPS

Ask butcher to cut chops about ¾ inch thick and to cut deep pockets into each chop.

8 thick lamb chops
FRESH HERB STUFFING
2 cups stale bread crumbs
½ cup finely chopped celery
½ cup seedless golden raisins
4 shallots, chopped
1 clove garlic, crushed
½ cup pine nuts, toasted
½ cup chopped fresh dill
¼ cup chopped fresh mint
2 tablespoons chopped parsley
1 oz butter, melted
MUSTARD BUTTER
2 oz butter, melted
2 tablespoons French mustard
1 tablespoon lemon juice
1 teaspoon dried rosemary leaves

Cut pockets into chops, push Fresh Herb Stuffing into pockets. Brush chops with Mustard Butter. Barbecue, brushing frequently with Mustard Butter.

Fresh Herb Stuffing: Combine all ingredients, mix well.

Mustard Butter: Combine all ingredients, beat until smooth.

Serves 8.

LAMB'S KIDNEYS WITH TOMATOES

8 lamb's kidneys
2 teaspoons French mustard
1 tablespoon barbecue sauce
1 clove garlic, crushed
1 cup dry white wine
4 tomatoes
1 tablespoon chopped parsley

Cut kidneys in half lengthwise. Remove hard core and any fat and sinew; rinse kidneys well, pat dry. Marinate kidneys in mustard, barbecue sauce, garlic and wine covered for several hours or refrigerate overnight. Cut tomatoes in half, barbecue quickly on both sides. Barbecue kidneys until just tender, turning once. Serve kidneys on top of tomatoes, sprinkle with parsley

Makes 8.

Chicken, etc.

All cuts of chicken barbecue well—and fast. Cook gently for best results. Duck, quail and game hen are also great successes on the barbecue.

CHICKEN WITH ORANGE CURRANT GLAZE

6 large chicken pieces
¼ cup red currant jelly
1 tablespoon grated orange rind
1 cup orange juice
1 teaspoon grated fresh ginger
¼ teaspoon dry mustard
1 tablespoon cornstarch
1 tablespoon water

Place chicken pieces in large dish. Heat jelly gently in pan until melted, add orange rind and juice, until melted, add orange rind and juice, ginger and mustard; pour over chicken. Marinate for several hours, or cover and refrigerate overnight. Barbecue chicken until cooked through and golden brown. Heat orange mixture in a pan, stir in blended cornstarch and water, stir until sauce boils and thickens. Serve over chicken.
    Serves 6.

CHICKEN DRUMSTICKS WITH CHILI BEANS

Chili seasoning mix is available in supermarkets in sachets.

12 chicken drumsticks
SPICY CHILI MIX
3 tablespoons dried oregano leaves
3 tablespoons paprika
1 teaspoon dry mustard
½ x 1½ chili seasoning mixes
1 teaspoon chili powder
2 teaspoons ground cumin
CHILI BEANS
½ oz butter
1 clove garlic, crushed
2 onions, chopped
2 green peppers, chopped
2 x 14-oz cans red kidney beans, drained
2 x 14 ½-oz cans tomatoes
⅓ cup tomato paste
½ x 1½ oz chili seasoning mixes
1 cup water
½ cup sliced stuffed olives

Simmer drumsticks in pan of water for 15 minutes, drain. Roll drumsticks in Spicy Chili Mix, cook on barbecue plate, turning and brushing with oil, until cooked through. Top with Chili Beans.
Spicy Chili Mix: Combine all ingredients in screw-top jar. Leftover mixture will keep for several months.
Chili Beans: Sauté garlic, onions, chili and peppers in butter few minutes. Add kidney beans, undrained crushed tomatoes, tomato paste, remaining chili seasoning mix and water. Simmer 30 minutes uncovered, stirring occasionally. Stir in olives just before serving.
    Serves 6.

DRUMSTICKS WITH BASIL BUTTER

12 chicken drumsticks
6 oz butter
¾ cup chopped fresh basil
1 tablespoon pine nuts, chopped
1 clove garlic, crushed
¼ cup grated Parmesan cheese

Bring pan of water to boil, add drumsticks, reduce heat, simmer 12 minutes; drain, cool. Beat softened butter in bowl with basil, pine nuts, garlic and Parmesan cheese. Spread a little butter mixture between flesh an skin of drumsticks. Barbecue drumsticks, basting frequently with butter mixture until cooked through.
    Serves 6.

TABBOULEH IN CHICKEN FILLETS WITH TOMATO SAUCE

Use the continental or Italian parsley for best flavor

8 chicken breast fillets
2 tablespoons oil
TABBOULEH STUFFING
¾ cup bulgur (cracked wheat)
½ cup finely chopped parsley
⅓ cup finely chopped mint
4 shallots, chopped
2 tablespoons oil
2 tablespoons lemon juice
pinch chili powder
TOMATO SAUCE
½ oz butter
1 small onion, finely chopped
14½-oz can tomatoes
1 tablespoon tomato paste
1 chicken stock cube

Cut a pocket in the side of each chicken fillet, fill with Tabbouleh mixture, secure opening with toothpicks. Barbecue, basting frequently with oil. Serve with Tomato Sauce.

Tabbouleh Stuffing: Soak bulgur in boiling water for about 30 minutes, strain; squeeze excess moisture out with hands. Combine bulgur, parsley, mint and shallots. Add combined oil, lemon juice and chili powder, mix well.

Tomato Sauce: Sauté onion in butter few minutes, add undrained crushed tomatoes, tomato paste and crumbled stock cube, simmer uncovered 10 minutes.

Serves 8.

CHICKEN FILLETS WITH MANGO CHUTNEY GLAZE

6 chicken breast fillets
1 tablespoon apricot jam
1 tablespoon mango chutney
½ cup mayonnaise
1 teaspoon Worcestershire sauce
2 teaspoons seeded mustard
1 tablespoon lemon juice

Pound chicken fillets lightly with mallet, place in dish, add combined jam, chutney, mayonnaise, Worcestershire sauce, mustard and lemon juice. Marinate several hours or overnight refrigerated. Barbecue chicken until cooked through, basting frequently with glaze.

Serves 6.

CHICKEN FILLETS IN GINGER LIME SAUCE

6 chicken breast fillets
black pepper
GINGER LIME SAUCE
½ cup brown sugar
¼ cup lime juice
2 tablespoons rum
3 teaspoons grated fresh ginger
2 cloves garlic, crushed
dash Tabasco sauce

Pound chicken lightly with mallet, season both sides with pepper. Barbecue until tender, basting frequently with Ginger Lime Sauce. Serve remaining Sauce separately.

Ginger Lime Sauce: Combine all ingredients, stir over heat without boiling until sugar is dissolved, bring Sauce to boil.

Serves 6.

SATAY CHICKEN
8 boneless chicken thighs
½ cup crunchy peanut butter
1 cup chicken stock
2 tablespoons dry sherry
1 tablespoon soy sauce
2 tablespoons lime or lemon juice
1 teaspoon grated fresh ginger
2 tablespoons honey
1 clove garlic, crushed
1 onion, finely chopped
2 teaspoons curry powder
1 teaspoon ground cumin
1 teaspoon ground coriander
dash Tabasco sauce

Cut chicken into strips 1 inch wide. Combine remaining ingredients in shallow dish, add chicken, mix well, cover, stand several hours or refrigerate overnight. Remove chicken from peanut mixture, place mixture into pan, bring to boil, reduce heat, simmer 15 minutes.

Thread 3 or 4 pieces of chicken onto skewers. Barbecue chicken, turning often, serve with peanut sauce.

Makes about 12 skewers.

CHICKEN WINGS TERIYAKI
4½ lb chicken wings
½ cup teriyaki sauce
2 tablespoons oil
1 teaspoon grated fresh ginger
2 cloves garlic, crushed
2 tablespoons dry sherry
2 tablespoons honey
¼ teaspoon sesame oil
½ teaspoon five-spice powder
1 tablespoon sesame seeds, toasted

Combine teriyaki sauce, oil, ginger, garlic, sherry, honey, sesame oil and five-spice powder in shallow dish. Add chicken wings, marinate covered for several hours, or refrigerate overnight, turning occasionally. Barbecue until cooked through. Baste while barbecuing with remaining marinade. Serve sprinkled with sesame seeds.

Serves 8.

CHICKEN WINGS WITH CURRY HONEY GLAZE
4½ lb chicken wings
¼ cup honey
2 teaspoons curry powder
2 teaspoons soy sauce
½ cup water
¼ cup oil

Place chicken wings in large dish. Combine honey, curry, soy sauce, water and oil in pan, heat until honey is melted, pour over chicken wings. Marinate for several hours or refrigerate overnight. Barbecue wings until cooked through. Baste frequently with honey mixture during barbecuing.

Serves 8.

CHICKEN AND PINEAPPLE KEBABS

8 boneless chicken thighs
1 fresh pineapple, peeled
1 red bell pepper
1 green bell pepper
1 tablespoon mint leaves
1 tablespoon honey
1 tablespoon oil
1 tablespoon lemon juice

Cut chicken, half the pineapple and the peppers into 1¼-inch pieces. Thread chicken, pineapple and pepper onto skewers. Blend or process remaining pineapple, mint leaves, honey, oil and lemon juice until smooth Brush some of the pineapple mixture over kebabs. Barbecue until chicken is cooked through. Serve pineapple mixture as a sauce.

Makes about 12 kebabs.

FRUITY CHICKEN LIVER KEBABS

1 cup dried apricots
12 oz chicken livers
1 tablespoon soy sauce
1 tablespoon honey
1 teaspoon grated fresh ginger
1 tablespoon oil
7 bacon slices
1 cup pitted prunes

Cover apricots with cold water, stand 30 minutes. Combine halved livers with soy sauce, honey and ginger, stand 30 minutes. Heat oil in pan or on barbecue plate, cook livers until lightly browned all over. Cut each bacon slice into 3 pieces crossways. Wrap each piece of liver in a piece of bacon. Skewer prunes, apricots and chicken rolls onto skewers. Brush lightly with oil, barbecue until bacon is cooked.

Makes about 10 kebabs.

PARSLEY-SEASONED CHICKEN

Prepare chicken a day before barbecuing if desired.

2¾-lb chicken
3 shallots, chopped
1 clove garlic, crushed
2 oz butter
1 cup stale bread crumbs
½ cup chopped parsley
4 oz butter, extra
1 tablespoon seeded mustard
1 clove garlic, crushed
2 teaspoons curry powder

Cut through breastbone of chicken, turn chicken over, flatten with hand or rolling pin. Sauté shallots and garlic in butter for 1 minute. Stir in bread crumbs and parsley. Loosen skin of chicken by sliding hand between skin and flesh of chicken at the neck joint. Push seasoning under skin, work it down to top of legs and across back. Combine extra butter with mustard, garlic and curry powder. Spread some of the butter over chicken, barbecue on both sides until cooked through; brush frequently with remaining butter during cooking.

Serves 4 to 6.

CORNISH HENS WITH APRICOT AND GINGER

3 x 1-lb Cornish hens
14-fl-oz can apricot nectar
2 teaspoons soy sauce
2 teaspoons grated fresh ginger
1 tablespoon apricot jam

Cut Cornish hens in half. Combine apricot nectar, soy sauce, ginger and jam in bowl, add Cornish hens, marinate several hours or refrigerate overnight. Remove hens, boil apricot mixture until reduced by half. Barbecue Cornish hens on both sides until cooked through, basting frequently with apricot mixture.

Serves 6.

MARINATED DUCK IN MANDARIN SAUCE

2 x 3-lb ducks
1 orange
2 x 10-oz cans mandarin segments
2 tablespoons brown sugar
1 cup dry white wine
1 chicken stock cube
½ cup hot water
1 clove garlic, crushed
1 teaspoon grated fresh ginger
2 tablespoons cornstarch
1 oz butter
2 tablespoons oil

Peel rind from orange, remove white pith; cut rind into fine strips, squeeze juice from orange, measure ½ cup juice.

Drain mandarins, reserve ½ cup syrup. Add syrup to pan with orange juice, brown sugar, wine, crumbled stock cube, hot water, garlic and ginger, stir over heat until sugar is dissolved. Quarter ducks, place in dish, pour marinade over, cover, stand 2 hours or refrigerate overnight.

Remove duck from marinade, barbecue, turning frequently until duck is tender and skin crisp. Baste frequently with combined melted butter and oil during barbecuing.

Blend cornstarch with some of the marinade, add remaining marinade, stir constantly until mixture boils and thickens. Add mandarins and orange rind, serve over hot duck.

Serves 8.

QUAIL WITH GRAPE STUFFING

Use 8 oz seedless grapes instead of canned grapes when in season.

8 quail
8 bacon slices
GRAPE STUFFING
½ oz butter
1 onion, finely chopped
2 cloves garlic, crushed
14 oz seedless green grapes, drained
1 cup stale bread crumbs
1 tablespoon chopped chives
½ teaspoon ground sage
black pepper

Fill cavity of quails with Grape Stuffing. Tie legs with string. Wrap a bacon slice around each quail to protect the breast from drying out during cooking, secure with toothpicks. Barbecue quail gently, turning frequently and basting with oil.

Grape Stuffing: Sauté onion and garlic in butter few minutes, place in bowl, add grapes, bread crumbs, chives, sage and black pepper, mix well.

Vegetables

Most of these vegetables are cooked in aluminum foil. Use a double thickness of foil.

TOMATOES WITH ZUCCHINI FILLING

6 tomatoes
4 shallots, chopped
1 clove garlic, crushed
1 oz butter
2 zucchini, grated
2 teaspoons tomato paste
1 tablespoon chopped fresh basil
1 tablespoon grated Parmesan
    cheese

Cut top from tomatoes, scoop out half the pulp; reserve. Sauté shallots and garlic in butter for 1 minute, add zucchini, tomato paste, basil and reserved tomato pulp; cook further 1 minute. Spoon filling into tomatoes, sprinkle with cheese, barbecue until heated through.
    Serves 6.

CHEESY VEGETABLES IN ZUCCHINI

6 medium zucchini
2 bacon slices, finely chopped
1 onion, finely chopped
1 clove garlic, crushed
2 teaspoons butter
1 tablespoon all-purpose flour
½ cup milk
1 cup grated tasty cheese
14½-oz can mixed vegetables,
    drained
1 tablespoon chopped fresh dill
1 tablespoon drained capers
2 tablespoons grated Parmesan
    cheese.

Add zucchini to pan of boiling water, boil 3 minutes, drain. Split in half lengthwise, scoop out pulp. Fry bacon until crisp, drain. Sauté onion and garlic in butter few minutes, add flour, cook 1 minute, stirring. Gradually stir in milk, stir until sauce boils and thickens. Add tasty cheese, vegetables, dill and capers. Fill zucchini with vegetable mixture, stand on heatproof tray, sprinkle with bacon and Parmesan cheese. Cover loosely with aluminum foil, barbecue until filling is hot.
    Serves 6.

ONIONS WITH CHICKEN AND CORN

6 medium onions
2 bacon slices, finely chopped
1 teaspoon curry powder
1½ cups finely chopped cooked
    chicken
14½-oz can creamed corn
1 small red bell pepper, finely
    chopped

Peel onions, leaving root end intact to hold onion together. Carefully pull centers from onions, leaving about three outside layers intact. Drop onions into pan of boiling water, boil for 3 minutes, drain upside down.
    Cook bacon with curry powder until bacon is crisp, drain. Add remaining ingredients; mix well. Fill onion shells with chicken mixture, wrap onions individually in aluminum foil. Barbecue until filling is heated through.
    Serves 6.

SURPRISE VEGETABLE PARCELS

Quick Cook wheat is available in super-markets. It almost triples in bulk after cooking.

2 bacon slices, chopped
3 cups cooked Quick Cook wheat or brown rice
2 tablespoons chopped parsley
3 carrots, quartered
18 baby squash
6 small pieces cauliflower
6 small pieces broccoli
2 oz butter
1 clove garlic, crushed
1 teaspoon dried basil leaves
1 cup grated tasty cheese

Cut 6 pieces of aluminum foil about 10x12 inches. Fry bacon until crisp, drain, combine with wheat and parsley, divide between foil pieces. Boil or steam vegetables until just starting to tenderize. Add them to pan in this order: carrots, squash, cauliflower, then broccoli. Do not cook more than 5 minutes, drain, divide over wheat mixture. Mix butter with garlic and basil, spread a little onto each parcel of vegetables, sprinkle with cheese. Wrap parcels tightly, barbecue until cheese is melted and vegetables are as tender as desired.
 Serves 6.

HONEY SWEET YAMS

3 medium yams, peeled
3 oz pecans
2 oz butter
1 teaspoon grated orange rind
1 cup orange juice
¼ cup honey
pinch cinnamon
2 tablespoons chopped chives

Chop yams into large cubes. Bring pan of water to boil, add potatoes, boil uncovered 5 to 10 minutes, or until yams are just tender; drain.
 Melt butter in pan, add pecans, cook stirring until pecans are lightly browned, remove from pan. Add orange rind, orange juice, honey and cinnamon to remaining butter in pan. Bring to boil, boil uncovered until liquid is reduced by half. Ad yams, cook, stirring, until heated through, stir in pecans and chives.
 Serves 6.

MUSHROOMS WITH LEMON HERB BUTTER

1 lb large mushrooms
4 oz butter
1 clove garlic, crushed
2 teaspoons grated lemon rind
½ cup chopped parsley
1 tablespoon chopped chives

Combine softened butter, garlic, lemon rind, parsley and chives. Remove stems from mushrooms, dot mushrooms with butter, cook on barbecue plate until heated through and butter melted.
 Serves 6.

CORN WITH PARMESAN MAYONNAISE
6 fresh corn cobs
butter
PARMESAN MAYONNAISE
2 egg yolks
2 teaspoons French mustard
1 clove garlic, crushed
1 tablespoon lemon juice
¾ cup oil
½ cup grated Parmesan cheese
½ cup cream
2 shallots, chopped

Remove corn husks and silks. Spread 6 pieces of aluminum foil with butter, wrap a cob of corn in each piece of foil, barbecue until tender, turning every 5 minutes. Top with Parmesan Mayonnaise.
Parmesan Mayonnaise: Combine egg yolks, mustard, garlic and lemon juice in food processor. With motor running, add oil very slowly through feed tube, add cheese and cream, process until combined, stir in shallots.
Serves 6.

CRAB-FILLED MUSHROOM CAPS
12 medium mushrooms
½ oz butter
1 stick celery
4-oz package cream cheese
1 tablespoon mayonnaise
2 teaspoons lime or lemon juice
1 teaspoon grated fresh ginger
dash Tabasco sauce
2 tablespoons chopped chives
2 tablespoons chopped red bell pepper
6-oz can crab, drained
2 tablespoons toasted flaked almonds

Remove stems from mushrooms, chop stems finely, sauté in butter with celery. Beat cream cheese and mayonnaise until smooth, stir in lime juice, ginger, Tabasco, chives, pepper and flaked crab. Fill caps with crab mixture, sprinkle with almonds. Barbecue until bottoms of mushrooms are browned and filling is hot.
Serves 6.

SALMON SOUR CREAM POTATOES
6 medium potatoes
7-oz can red salmon, drained
1 tablespoon sour cream
3 shallots, chopped
1 gherkin, chopped

Boil or steam potatoes until tender; drain, cool slightly. Cut top from each potato, scoop out inside pulp and mash well. Combine mashed potato with salmon, sour cream, shallots and gherkin. Spoon filling into potatoes, place each potato on a piece of aluminum foil, wrap securely. Barbecue until heated through. Top with extra sour cream if desired.
Serves 6.

CHEESY SPINACH POTATOES
6 medium potatoes
8-oz package frozen spinach
½ cup grated Parmesan cheese
2 shallots, chopped
¼ teaspoon nutmeg

Boil or steam potatoes until tender; drain, cool slightly. Cut top from each potato, scoop out inside pulp and mash well. Place spinach in dry pan, cook until thawed and all liquid evaporated. Add cheese, shallots, nutmeg and mashed potato to spinach, mix well. Spoon filling into potatoes, place each potato on a piece of aluminum foil, wrap securely. Barbecue until heated through.
Serves 6.

Breads

Bring some hot, homemade bread out to the barbecue and watch it disappear rapidly. The French Bread Sticks and Whole-Grain Bread need normal preparation, but the other three recipes are quick and easy.

WHOLE-WHEAT CORN BREAD

2½ cups whole-wheat flour
1 envelope rapid-rise dry yeast
1 teaspoon sugar
¼ teaspoon salt
1 x 12 oz can Mexicorn, undrained
⅓ cup milk
4 oz butter
1 egg, lightly beaten

In large bowl, combine flour, yeast, sugar and salt. In medium saucepan, combine Mexicorn, milk and butter; heat just until warm and butter melts. Stir corn mixture into flour. Add egg. Knead lightly until thoroughly combined. Roll mixture into 12 rounds and place in greased 9-inch deep round cake pan. Cover with plastic wrap. Let stand in warm place 45 minutes. Bake in 400° oven 45 minutes. Serve warm with butter.

WHOLE-GRAIN BREAD

3¾ cups whole-wheat flour
1¾ cups all-purpose flour
¼ oz package dry yeast
2 tablespoons sugar
2 cups warm water
⅓ cup bulgur (cracked wheat)
1 teaspoon salt
½ oz butter
GLAZE
1 egg white
1 tablespoon water

Combine sifted flours in large bowl; return husks in sifter to bowl. Combine yeast and sugar in small bowl, stir in 1 cup water. Add to well in center of dry ingredients, stand covered in a warm place until liquid starts to bubble, up to 10 minutes. Stir some of the flour into yeast mixture, add bulgur, salt and butter, mix in with remaining water; mix to a firm dough. Cover bowl with plastic food wrap, stand in warm place for 15 minutes. Turn onto a lightly floured surface, knead well for 10 minutes, incorporating as little flour as possible from board. Place in bowl, cover with plastic food wrap, stand in warm place for 1 hour. Turn onto floured surface; shape into 2 loaves, place into 2 greased 8x4x3-inch loaf pans. Stand in warm place until doubled in bulk, about 30 minutes. Brush tops with Glaze. Bake in hot oven 15 minutes, reduce heat to moderate, bake further 15 minutes. Remove bread, carefully from pans, place on oven rack, bake further 10 minutes or until crust is well browned.

AUSTRALIAN PUMPKIN DAMPER

You will need about 3¼ lb pumpkin to get 3 cups mashed pumpkin; do not use milk, cream, butter, etc., when mashing. Use an old, dry pumpkin, not the soft butternut variety.

2¼ lb self-rising flour
½ teaspoon salt
2 oz butter
3 cups mashed pumpkin
⅓ cup water, approximately

Sift flour and salt into bowl, rub in butter. Make well in center of dry ingredients, add mashed pumpkin and enough water to mix to a sticky dough. Turn onto lightly floured surface; knead lightly until smooth, cut in half. Knead each piece of dough gently into round shape, place onto 2 lightly greased oven trays. Pat dough out to a 6-inch circle. Cut a cross in top of each damper about ¼ inch deep, sift a little extra flour over each one. Bake in hot oven 10 minutes, reduce heat to moderate, bake further 20 to 30 minutes. Alternate position of dampers in oven halfway through cooking time.

Makes 2 dampers.

FRENCH BREAD STICKS

1½ oz compressed yeast
1 teaspoon sugar
2 teaspoons butter
1¼ cups warm water
4 cups all purpose flour
1 teaspoon salt
1 egg
sesame or poppy seeds

Stir yeast and sugar together until liquid, add butter and warm water, stir until butter is melted. Sift flour and salt into large bowl, make a well in center, pour in yeast mixture, stir flour gradually into liquid. Turn onto lightly floured surface, knead 10 minutes or until dough is smooth and elastic. Place dough into greased bowl, cover with plastic food wrap, stand in warm place for 1 to 1½ hours, or until dough has doubled in bulk. Turn dough onto floured surface, knead 2 minutes. Roll dough into 8x12-inch rectangle, cut in half lengthwise. Roll up each half as tightly as possible from the long side, tuck in ends, place on greased oven trays. Cover loosely with plastic food wrap, put in warm place to rise for 20 minutes. Cut deep slashes in each loaf, brush lightly with beaten egg, sprinkle with sesame or poppy seeds. Bake in moderately hot oven 20 minutes, sprinkle with water, bake further 10 minutes or until golden brown.

Makes 2 loaves

EGG AND CHUTNEY SLICE

Use chutney of your choice. Prepare the Slice up to 12 hours before serving. If desired, cover, refrigerate, bake as directed when ready to serve.

2 cups self-rising flour
1 oz butter
½ cup milk, approximately
1 cup grated cheddar cheese
FILLING
1 onion, finely chopped
1 oz butter
¼ cup chutney
3 hard-boiled eggs, chopped

Rub butter into sifted flour, add enough milk to mix to a sticky dough. Knead dough lightly on floured surface, cut in half. Roll out half the dough large enough to cover base of greased 10x12-inch swiss roll pan. Spread with Filling, cover with remaining piece of rolled-out dough. Sprinkle with cheese. Mark into squares by cutting through top layer of biscuit dough. Bake in moderately hot oven 20 to 30 minutes or until golden brown. Place onto wire rack, cut into squares, serve hot or cold, split and buttered, if desired.

Filling: Heat butter in pan, add onion, sauté until transparent, cool few minutes, mix in chutney and eggs.

Top: French Bread Sticks; Center: Pumpkin Damper, Whole-wheat Corn Bread; bottom: Egg and Chutney Slice; Whole-Grain Bread.

Savory Butters

Serve generous pats of these butters on hot sizzling steaks. Butters can be made up to a month in advance and frozen. Shape the frozen butter into a log and roll tightly in freezer wrap, then in aluminum foil. Cut off slices as required.

40

HERB MUSTARD BUTTER
8 oz unsalted butter
½ cup finely chopped parsley
2 tablespoons chopped chives
3 teaspoons French mustard
2 teaspoons lemon juice
Beat softened butter with remaining ingredients until combined.

ANCHOVY BUTTER
8 oz unsalted butter
1½-oz can flat anchovy fillets, drained
1 clove garlic, crushed
2 tablespoons grated Parmesan cheese
1 teaspoon lemon juice
Beat softened butter with remaining ingredients until combined.

ROQUEFORT BUTTER
4 oz unsalted butter
4-oz package cream cheese
3-oz package Roquefort cheese
2 teaspoons lemon juice
Beat softened butter and cream cheese together until smooth. Add Roquefort cheese and lemon juice, continue beating until combined.

Seafood

Seafood is becoming popular to serve at a barbecue. Don't overcook or it will become dry and tough. Shellfish and squid are best cooked rapidly over a high heat.

GARLIC SHRIMP
3¼ lb large green shrimp
3 cups oil
6 oz butter
12 cloves garlic
3 small chiles
1 tablespoon chopped parsley

Shell shrimp, leaving tail intact, remove back vein. Put ½ cup oil into 6 individual fireproof dishes, add 1 oz butter to each dish. Crush 2 cloves of garlic into each dish. Seed and finely chop red chiles, divide evenly among dishes. Put dishes on barbecue, heat until butter has melted and oil is very hot. Divide shrimp between dishes, heat until shrimp are cooked. Serve immediately, sprinkle with parsley.
   Serves 6.

MUSSELS IN FRESH TOMATO SAUCE

2¼ lb mussels
1 onion, chopped
2 cloves garlic, crushed
2 tablespoons oil
2¼ lb ripe tomatoes, chopped
¾ cup chicken stock
½ cup dry white wine
½ teaspoon dried oregano leaves
2 tablespoons tomato paste
¼ cup chopped parsley

Sauté onion and garlic in oil until tender. Add tomatoes, chicken stock, wine, oregano and tomato paste. Bring to boil, reduce heat, simmer 30 minutes, cover. Puree sauce or push through sieve. Scrub mussels under cold water. Return sauce to pan, place on barbecue, bring to boil, add mussels, cover, simmer 5 to 7 minutes or until mussels open; sprinkle with parsley.

Serves 6.

LOBSTER TAILS WITH LEMON BUTTER

If preferred, make this recipe using lime juice instead of lemon.

3 oz butter, melted
3 tablespoons lemon juice
3 tablespoons honey
2 tablespoons chopped chives
1 tablespoon chopped fresh dill
6 lobster tails

Combine melted butter with lemon juice, honey, chives and dill. Cut soft fins and shell away from underside of lobster tails. Brush lobster tails with lemon butter, barbecue until cooked and tender. Brush with lemon butter while cooking.

Serves 6.

BARBECUED TROUT WITH PINE NUT FILLING

4 whole trout
2 gherkins
PINE NUT FILLING
2 bacon slices, chopped
¼ cup pine nuts
2 tablespoons chopped chives
3 shallots, chopped
2 cups stale bread crumbs
¼ cup sour cream

Trim fins from cleaned fish. Open fish out as flat as possible, skin side up. Run rolling pin firmly down backbone, starting from tail. Turn trout over, with a sharp knife cut through backbone at each end of fish. Gently lever backbone out, remove any remaining bones. Fill cavity of fish with Pine Nut Filling. Place each trout on greased sheet of aluminum foil. Slice gherkins into fine strips; sprinkle over trout. Fold aluminum foil over top and seal ends completely. Barbecue until fish are tender

Pine Nut Filling: Fry bacon until crisp, add pine nuts, fry 1 minute more; drain. Stir in remaining ingredients.

Serves 6.

SNAPPER WITH SAFFRON RICE

2¼ lb whole snapper
SAFFRON RICE FILLING
½ cup long-grain rice
¼ teaspoon saffron threads
1 cup water
½ oz butter
2 cloves garlic, crushed
2 shallots, chopped
1 stick celery, finely chopped
6-oz can crab, drained

Run knife inside fish across bones, starting from head and working down to tail to remove bones. Do not cut through back. Turn fish, repeat on other side, cut center bone at both ends, gently lift bone out. Spread Saffron Rice Filling evenly inside fish. Brush fish on both sides with oil Barbecue wrapped in foil or placed in wire basket.

Saffron Rice Filling: Place rice, saffron and water in pan, bring to boil, reduce heat, simmer gently uncovered 12 minutes or until water has evaporated. Cover, stand 10 minutes. Melt butter in pan, add garlic, shallots and celery, sauté 1 minute, stir in crabmeat and rice.

Serves 2.

MARINATED SQUID WITH WHIPPED CUCUMBER SAUCE

2¼ lb cleaned squid
½ cup dry red wine
1 tablespoon lemon or lime juice
¼ cup oil
¼ cup French dressing
½ teaspoon dried basil leaves

WHIPPED CUCUMBER SAUCE
1 small cucumber
½ x 8-oz carton sour cream
2 teaspoons lime or lemon juice
½ x 8-oz carton whipping cream
2 teaspoons chopped fresh dill
1 tablespoon chopped chives

Cut squid into rings, place in dish, add red wine, lemon juice, oil, French dressing and basil, cover, stand for 1 to 2 hours. Barbecue in batches on hot greased plate for about 30 seconds.

Whipped Cucumber Sauce: Peel and seed cucumber, sprinkle with salt. Place in strainer, stand 15 minutes. Rinse under cold water, pat dry. Blend or process cucumber with sour cream and lime juice until smooth. Whip cream until soft peaks form, fold in cucumber puree, dill and chives.

Serves 6.

FISH CUTLETS WITH PROVENCALE SAUCE

6 fish cutlets
MARINADE
1 onion, grated
1 cup dry white wine
½ cup oil
1 tablespoon lemon juice
2 cloves garlic, crushed
2 tablespoons finely chopped
    parsley
1 bay leaf

PROVENCALE SAUCE
4 tomatoes, peeled, chopped
1 oz butter
1 tablespoon tomato paste
½ teaspoon sugar
½ teaspoon dried oregano leaves
2 oz black olives, pitted, chopped
1 small green pepper, chopped
4 shallots, chopped

Place cutlets in single layer in dish, add Marinade, cover, refrigerate 1 to 2 hours. Barbecue, basting with Marinade, until fish is just tender. Serve with sauce.

Marinade: Combine all ingredients.

Provencale Sauce: Cook tomatoes in butter few minutes, add tomato paste, sugar, oregano, black olives and pepper, simmer uncovered 5 minutes. Stir in shallots just before serving.

Serves 6.

CHILI SHRIMP

3¼ lb large green shrimp
⅓ cup oil
1½ tablespoons honey
1½ tablespoons chili sauce
1 tablespoon lemon juice
4 shallots, finely chopped
2 tablespoons chopped parsley
¼ teaspoon five-spice powder

Shell shrimp, leave tails intact, remove back vein. Combine remaining ingredients in bowl, mix well; mix in shrimp, cover, refrigerate 1 to 2 hours. Thread shrimp onto skewers, barbecue quickly until cooked and tender. Brush with remaining marinade during cooking.

Serves 6.

SEAFOOD KEBABS WITH LIME DILL BUTTER

Make Lime Dill Butter two days before required, keep refrigerated. Return to room temperature before using.

2¼ lb large green shrimp
8 oz scallops
4 limes
LIME DILL BUTTER
2 egg yolks
1 teaspoon grated lime rind
1 tablespoon lime juice
4 oz butter
1 tablespoon chopped fresh dill

Peel and devein shrimp, leaving tail intact. Thread shrimp, scallops and lime wedges onto skewers. Barbecue until cooked through, serve with Lime Dill Butter.

Lime Dill Butter: Place egg yolks, lime rind and juice in top of double saucepan, stir over simmering water 1 minute. Whisk in small pieces of softened butter gradually, whisk until sauce thickens. Remove from heat, stir in dill, cool to room temperature.

Serves 6.

A relaxed and chatty brunch is one of the most pleasant ways to entertain friends or to put the family in a togetherness mood. In summer, brunch can begin as early as 9 A.M. If company and conversation are good, it can easily go on until late afternoon. To make your brunch go smoothly, you will need some dishes that can be prepared a day or so ahead. Our flans and roulades and, among first courses, Fruity Swiss Müesli and Old-Fashioned Apple Cobbler are ideal. Many dishes, however, must be cooked a moment or two before they are eaten. Do this at the table if you feel that you can do so successfully, or sometimes a guest is willing to take over. Most egg dishes, such as omelets, Eggs Florentine, Eggs Benedict and scrambles come into the last-moment category. Check your ingredients for these well in advance. We have, however, included Eggs and Bacon Rolls and Ham and Cheese Puffs, which may be prepared several hours ahead.

Accompaniments to a good brunch include a choice of pure fruit juices, good tea and coffee, which you can serve iced in summer. If the brunch goes beyond the middle of the day, there is nothing nicer than chilled dry white wine or champagne, or even a punch.

Back from left: Spiral Herb Bread, page 63; Fruity Swiss Müesli, page 49; Croissants, page 60. Center from left: Potato Cheese Scramble, page 50; Strawberries and Oranges with Honey Yogurt Topping, page 48; Avocado and Bacon Omelet, page 55; Spinach and Cottage Cheese Flan, page 58. Front from left: Crispy Potato Fritters, page 64; Leek and Watercress Flan, page 58; Blinis with Smoked Salmon and Caviar, page 55.

Fruits

Choose two or three varieties of fruity dishes to serve—also a selection of fresh fruit. Melon balls—made with a melon baller and spiked with a toothpick—are light and easy to eat. Choose melons in season—mix and match the colors for a pretty effect. We chose honeydew and cantaloupe. These recipes serve ten. To give a wider choice to your guests, you might like to make half quantities of three or four of the recipes.

STRAWBERRIES AND ORANGES WITH HONEY-YOGURT TOPPING

1½ lb strawberries
3 large oranges
¼ cup Grand Marnier
HONEY-YOGURT TOPPING
½ pint whipping cream
6½ oz natural yogurt
¼ cup honey

Slice stawberries and oranges, add Grand Marnier, cover, refrigerate overnight or for several hours. Top with Honey-Yogurt Topping.

Honey-Yogurt Topping: Whip cream until beginning to thicken. Beat in honey, beat until thick. Fold in yogurt. Refrigerate overnight or for several hours.

Serves 10.

Right: Strawberries and Oranges with Honey Yogurt Topping; Grapefruit Cups; Melon Balls; Fruity Swiss Müesli.

GRAPEFRUIT CUPS

5 grapefruit
4 oranges
1 pineapple
3 passion fruit
HONEY SYRUP
½ cup honey
¾ cup water
1 cinnamon stick

Cut grapefruit in half crossways, scoop pulp out, taking care not to damage skin. Cut grapefruit pulp into segments. Peel oranges thickly, cut into segments. Peel pineapple, cut into small cubes. Combine grape fruit, orange, pineapple and passion fruit pulp in bowl. Divide fruit mixture evenly between grapefruit cups. Refrigerate until ready to serve, then top with Honey Syrup.

Honey Syrup: Combine honey, water and cinnamon stick in pan. Bring to boil, reduce heat, simmer gently uncovered for 5 minutes.

Serves 10.

FRUITY SWISS MÜESLI

This is a moist müesli—a nice change from the dry variety.

1 cup wheat germ
1 cup old-fashioned rolled oats
2 cups apple juice
2 tablespoons lemon juice
½ cup honey
2 apples
2 pears
1 lb seedless grapes
1 cup roasted hazelnuts, chopped

Combine wheat germ, rolled oats and apple juice. Cover, refrigerate overnight. Stir in lemon juice, honey, coarsely grated unpeeled apples, finely chopped unpeeled pears, halved grapes and hazelnuts.

Serves 10.

OLD-FASHIONED APPLE COBBLER

8 green apples, peeled and sliced
½ cup sugar
½ cup orange juice
2 cups old-fashioned rolled oats
½ cup all-purpose flour
½ teaspoon cinnamon
¼ teaspoon nutmeg
⅓ cup coarsely chopped walnuts
4 oz butter
¼ cup honey

Arrange apples in slightly overlapping layer over base of large greased baking dish. Sprinkle evenly with sugar, pour over orange juice. Combine oats, sifted flour, cinnamon, nutmeg and walnuts in bowl, mix well. Heat butter and honey in pan, add to oats, mix well. Sprinkle evenly over apples. Bake in moderate oven 40 minutes or until golden brown and crisp. Serve hot or cold with whipped cream.

Serves 10.

FRUIT COMPOTE

If serving cold, prepare the day before required and refrigerate. If serving hot, combine all ingredients and cook, then serve. We like to serve whipped cream or yogurt with our Compote.

3 pears
8 oz pitted prunes
8 oz dried apricots
4 oz seedless raisins
4 oz dried apples
4 oz dried figs
½ cup port
1¾ cups water
1½ cups orange juice
2 tablespoons sugar
½ cinnamon stick

Peel and dice pears, combine in pan with remaining ingredients. Bring to boil, reduce heat, simmer covered 30 minutes. Discard cinnamon stick.

Serves 10.

CRUNCHY CINNAMON CUBES WITH ORANGES

Grate an orange first for the 2 teaspoons grated orange rind required for the recipe.

10 oranges
2 teaspoons grated orange rind
8 slices white bread
4 oz butter
½ teaspoon cinnamon
2 tablespoons sugar
5 kiwifruit, peeled and sliced

Peel oranges and cut into segments. Remove crusts from bread, cut bread into small cubes. Melt butter in pan, add bread, stir constantly until golden brown and crisp all over. Add cinnamon, orange rind and sugar, stir further 1 minute. Serve with orange segments and sliced kiwifruit.

Serves 10.

Left: Fruit Compote; Crunchy Cinnamon Cubes with Oranges; Old-Fashioned Apple Cobbler.

Eggs

Here are four pages of splendid egg recipes, plus three great recipes for omelets. Some are best suited to a substantial late breakfast, but others, such as the classic Eggs Florentine and Eggs Benedict, are perfect for a luncheon main course.

POTATO CHEESE SCRAMBLE

Cook potatoes about an hour before serving. Scramble egg mixture as close to serving time as possible, or cook dish at the table.

3 potatoes, peeled
oil for shallow frying
2 onions, slice
1 green bell pepper, chopped
10 eggs
¼ cup cream
¼ teaspoon dried oregano leaves
1 cup grated cheddar cheese

Cut potatoes into ¾-inch cubes. Heat oil in pan, add potatoes, fry, stirring until golden brown all over; drain on kitchen paper. Pour off excess oil, leaving about a tablespoon in pan. Heat oil, add onions, fry until lightly browned; add pepper, cook few minutes, stirring. Drain away excess oil. Beat eggs with cream and oregano, add to pan with potatoes, onions and pepper. Stir constantly over low heat until mixture is just beginning to set. Remove from heat, lightly stir in cheese.

Serves 10.

HAM AND CHEESE PUFFS

Prepare Puffs up to several hours before baking. Bake only when ready to serve; they sink a little on cooling.

10 slices square sandwich ham
2 onions, finely chopped
1 oz butter
2 cups finely grated tasty cheese
10 eggs
2 x 6-oz cartons natural yogurt
2 tablespoons chopped parsley

Using ham, line 10 greased ovenproof dishes of 1-cup capacity. Sauté onions in butter until tender, divide evenly into ham-lined dishes, sprinkle evenly with half the cheese.

Beat eggs and yogurt together, pour into dishes. Sprinkle with remaining combined cheese and parsley. Stand on oven tray, bake in moderate oven 30 minutes. Turn out immediately, invert onto serving plates.

Serves 10.

EGG AND BACON ROLLS

Prepare and wrap several hours before cooking.

10 round crisp bread rolls
10 spinach leaves, chopped
1 oz butter
2 onions, chopped
4 bacon slices, diced
3 tablespoons barbecue sauce
10 eggs
1 cup grated cheddar cheese

Cut slice from top of bread rolls and reserve. Scoop out inside of bread rolls leaving a thin shell. Drop spinach into pan of boiling water, boil 1 minute; drain. Sauté spinach in hot butter for 1 minute; drain, divide spinach between bread rolls. Sauté onions and bacon in pan until tender, stir in barbecue sauce, spoon over spinach. Break eggs into each bread roll, top with cheese and replace lids. Wrap bread rolls in aluminum foil, stand on tray, bake in moderate oven 15 minutes. Remove from oven, stand 5 minutes before removing foil.

Serves 10.

SMOKED SALMON SCRAMBLE

Cook at the table or as close to serving time as possible.

4 oz package cream cheese
2 oz butter
½ cup cream
10 eggs
5 slices smoked salmon, chopped
1 tablespoon chopped capers
2 tablespoons chopped fresh dill

Cream cheese with butter and cream, place in pan over low heat, break eggs into pan, stir constantly with wooden spoon until mixture is smooth. Add smoked salmon, capers and dill, stir until eggs are just cooked and creamy.

Serves 10.

Back from left: Egg and Bacon Rolls; Potato Cheese Scramble.
Front from left: Smoked Salmon Scramble; Ham and Cheese Puffs.

Eggs Benedict and Florentine require organization to get them served hot. Practice with two eggs before you attempt ten. Use a large pan to poach the eggs, and be careful that the eggs are not overcooked.

EGGS FLORENTINE
10 poached eggs
10 spinach leaves, chopped
3 oz butter
3 tablespoons all-purpose flour
1 cup milk
½ cup cream
½ cup grated cheddar cheese
3 tablespoons grated Parmesan
    cheese

Place spinach in pan with only water left clinging to leaves after washing. Cook few minutes until soft, drain, toss with 1 oz of butter.

Heat remaining butter in pan, add flour, stir until smooth, cook 1 minute. Gradually add milk, stir until smooth, stir over heat until sauce boils and thickens, add cream and cheese, stir over heat until cheese melts.

To serve, divide spinach between 10 heatproof plates, make hollow in center of spinach, place a poached egg in each hollow, spoon hot sauce over eggs, sprinkle with Parmesan, grill until cheese is melted.

Serves 10.

EGGS BENEDICT SPECIAL
10 slices bacon
2 red bell peppers, sliced
2 green bell peppers, sliced
2 medium onions, sliced
5 English muffins, split and toasted
10 poached eggs
BLENDER HOLLANDAISE SAUCE
4 oz butter
3 egg yolks
1 teaspoon French mustard
2 teaspoons lemon juice
freshly ground black pepper

Blender Hollandaise Sauce: Melt butter over low heat. Beat egg yolks, mustard, lemon juice and pepper in blender, gradually blend in hot, melted butter while processor is operating.

Fry bacon until lightly browned. While still warm, roll up bacon, secure with toothpicks.

Leave about 3 tablespoons of bacon drippings in pan, add peppers and onions, sauté until tender.

To serve, spoon cooked pepper mixture onto toasted muffin halves on serving plates, top with poached eggs, then Sauce. Remove toothpicks from bacon, top each egg with a bacon roll. Place in moderately hot oven for a few minutes before serving.

Serves 10.

HAM AND CHEESE BAKED EGGS

Prepare several hours before baking.

3 oz butter
½ cup all-purpose flour
2½ cups milk
1½ cups grated cheddar cheese
4 oz ham, chopped
2 tablespoons chopped parsley
6 eggs

Melt butter in pan, add flour, stir over heat for 1 minute. Add milk gradually, stir until sauce boils and thickens. Remove from heat, add cheese, ham and parsley. Spread mixture evenly over base of shallow ovenproof dish to a depth of about 1 inch. Make six indentations with back of spoon in sauce, break an egg into each one. Bake in moderately hot oven 10 minutes or until eggs are set.

Serves 6.

CREAMY CURRIED EGGS

Prepare sauce up to a day before required. Add parsley just before heating. Boil eggs several hours beforehand.

15 hard-boiled eggs
SAUCE
2 oz butter
½ cup all-purpose flour
3 cups milk
½ pint cream
2 tablespoons mango chutney
2 teaspoons curry powder
½ cup chopped parsley

Melt butter in pan, add flour and stir over heat for 1 minute. Gradually stir in milk and cream, bring to boil, stirring until thickened. Reduce heat, add chutney, curry powder and parsley, simmer 10 minutes, uncovered. To serve, slice eggs, arrange over toast, top with Sauce.

Serves 10.

Omelets

Omelets are not difficult to make. All you require is a good pan and fast heat and you will be able to turn them out rapidly with just a tiny bit of practice. Swish the egg mixture quickly over the hot greased pan and draw the outside edges of the mixture into the center. Do this only until the eggs are just set; overcooking means a tough omelet. Remember, the omelet will cook a little more from its own heat, from a filling or if placed under broiler.

SMOKED WHITEFISH AND PEPPER OMELET

Make two of these omelets to serve ten.

1 lb smoked whitefish
1 red bell pepper, chopped
1 green bell pepper, chopped
1 clove garlic, crushed
1 oz butter
2 tablespoons lemon juice
6 eggs
⅓ cup grated cheddar cheese

Place fish in pan covered with water, bring to boil, reduce heat, simmer 10 minutes; drain and flake it with fork. Sauté peppers and garlic in butter, add fish and lemon juice, cook 1 minute. Heat greased omelet pan, add beaten eggs. Using a fork, draw eggs from side of pan into center, allow eggs to set evenly over low heat. When almost set, spoon fish mixture over top, sprinkle with cheese. Place under hot broiler to set top and melt cheese; do not overcook. Serve immediately cut into wedges.

AVOCADO AND BACON OMELET
10 oz sour cream
½ cup grated cheddar cheese
¼ cup chopped parsley
10 bacon slices
20 eggs
5 oz butter
3 avocados, sliced
Combine sour cream with cheese and parsley, mix well. Fry bacon until crisp and golden brown, drain, cut into ¾-inch pieces. Beat 2 eggs with fork until frothy. Heat omelet pan, add ½ oz of the butter to pan, add the 2 beaten eggs. Cook until eggs are just set. Spread tablespoonful of sour cream mixture over half of omelet. Top with bacon and avocado. Fold omelet over to cover filling. Slide onto serving dish. Repeat with the remaining eggs and filling to make 9 more omelets.

HAM OMELET WITH CHEESE SAUCE
1¼ lb ham
1 oz butter
3 onions, sliced
3 teaspoons French mustard
20 eggs
1 cup chopped parsley
5 oz butter, extra
CHEESE SAUCE
2 oz butter
2 tablespoons all-purpose flour
2 cups milk
½ cup cream
1 cup grated cheddar cheese
Cut ham into narrow strips. Melt butter in pan, add onion, cook until transparent, mix in ham and mustard.

Beat 2 eggs with about 1 tablespoon of the parsley with fork until frothy. Heat omelet pan, add ½ oz of the extra butter to pan. Pour egg mixture into pan, cook until mixture is just set, spoon tablespoonful of ham filling on half the omelet. Fold omelet over to cover filling. Slide onto serving dish. Repeat with remaining eggs, parsley and filling to make 9 more omelets. Spoon Cheese Sauce over just before serving.
Cheese Sauce: Melt butter in pan, stir in flour, cook 1 minute. Gradually stir in milk, stir until mixture boils and thickens. Add cream and cheese, stir until cheese is melted.

Pancakes

The pancakes for the Smoked Trout and the Layered Mushroom and Tomato Pancakes can be made up to two weeks in advance. Layer pancakes with plastic food wrap, wrap to keep airtight, freeze.

BLINIS WITH SMOKED SALMON AND CAVIAR

These pancakes do not freeze and reheat well. Have the mixture ready about an hour before the guests are due. Stack the pancakes, cover with foil and keep warm.

1 cup all-purpose flour
1 cup buckwheat flour
1 teaspoon salt
2 teaspoons dry yeast
1½ cups milk
3 eggs, separated
10 oz whipping cream

Front: Blinis with Smoked Salmon and Caviar. Back from left: Layered Mushroom and Tomato Pancakes; Smoked Trout Pancakes with Sour Cream and Cucumber Sauce.

Sift flour, buckwheat flour and salt into bowl, return husks from sifter to bowl; mix in yeast. Make well in center of dry ingredients, add combined warm milk and egg yolks, mix to a smooth batter. Cover bowl, stand in warm place for 1 hour or until mixture is light and frothy. Fold lightly whipped cream into batter. Beat egg whites until soft peaks form, gently fold into batter, cover, stand further 15 minutes.

Heat crepe pan, grease well. Pour about 3 tablespoons of batter into pan, cook over medium heat until bubbles appear on surface, turn blini over, cook other side until light golden brown. Repeat with remaining batter. Serve hot, topped with sour cream and accompanied by caviar and smoked salmon.

Makes about 15.

LAYERED MUSHROOM AND TOMATO PANCAKES

Prepare filling a day ahead. Pancakes may be layered, as directed in recipe, up to several hours before baking.

PANCAKES
1 cup all-purpose flour
3 eggs
1 cup milk
1 tablespoon oil
MUSHROOM FILLING
12 oz button mushrooms, sliced
6 shallots, chopped
1½ oz butter
1 teaspoon cornstarch
1 tablespoon sour cream
TOMATO FILLING
1 onion, chopped
1 oz butter
14½-oz can tomatoes
1 teaspoon cornstarch
1 teaspoon water

Sift flour into bowl, gradually stir in combined eggs and milk, beat until smooth. Stir in oil, stand 30 minutes. Heat pan, grease lightly. Pour about 3 tablespoons of batter into pan, cook until browned underneath, turn over and cook other side. Repeat with remaining batter. Place one pancake in ovenproof dish, spread small amount of Mushroom Filling over pancake, top with another pancake. Spread small amount of Tomato Filling over pancake, top with another pancake. Repeat until all pancakes are layered. Cover with aluminum foil, bake in moderate oven 10 to 15 minutes or until heated through. To serve, cut into wedges.

Mushroom Filling: Sauté mushrooms and shallots in butter 3 minutes. Add blended cornstarch and sour cream, stir until thickened.

Tomato Filling: Sauté onion in butter until tender. Add drained chopped tomatoes, cook 2 minutes. Add blended cornstarch and water, stir until thickened.

Serves 6.

SMOKED TROUT PANCAKES WITH SOUR CREAM AND CUCUMBER SAUCE

Prepare Filling up to two days before using, the Sauce one day before. Sauce will thicken, add a little milk to bring back to correct consistency. Remember the heat from the pancakes will melt the Sauce.

PANCAKES
1 cup all-purpose flour
3 eggs
1 cup milk
1 tablespoon oil
FILLING
3 smoked trout
4 shallots, chopped
1 stick celery, chopped
1 oz butter
6 oz cream cheese
2 tablespoons lemon juice

SAUCE
10 oz sour cream
1 tablespoon lemon juice
½ teaspoon French mustard
½ cucumber

Pancakes: Sift flour into bowl, gradually add combined eggs and milk, beat until smooth. Stir in oil; stand 30 minutes. Heat pan, grease lightly. Pour about 3 tablespoons batter into pan, cook until brown underneath, turn over and cook other side. Repeat with remaining batter. Spoon small amount of Filling onto pancake and roll up. Bake, covered, in lightly greased ovenproof dish 15 minutes. Serve with Sauce.

Filling: Place trout in pan, cover with water, bring to boil, reduce heat and simmer 10 minutes, turning once. Remove skin and bones from trout; discard. Sauté shallots and celery in butter. Beat cream cheese until soft, add other ingredients, beat until combined.

Sauce: Combine sour cream, lemon juice and French mustard. Peel cucumber, cut in half lengthwise, scrape out seeds with teaspoon. Cut cucumber into thin slices and add to Sauce.

Makes 12 pancakes.

Roulades

Roulades can be made several hours ahead. Reheat, covered with foil, in moderate oven. Each roulade yields about eight slices.

SPINACH AND SALMON ROULADE
2 oz butter
⅓ cup all-purpose flour
1 cup milk
4 eggs, separated
8-oz packet frozen spinach
FILLING
2 x 7½-oz cans red salmon, drained
4 shallots, chopped
½ cup mayonnaise
1 tablespoon chopped chives

Place frozen spinach in pan, cook over moderate heat until all liquid has evaporated. Melt butter in separate pan, add flour, stir 1 minute. Add milk gradually, stir until mixture boils and thickens. Quickly stir in egg yolks and spinach, transfer mixture to large bowl. Beat egg white until soft peaks form, fold lightly into spinach mixture. Pour mixture into greased and greaseproof paper–lined Swiss roll pan (base measures 10 inches). Bake in hot oven 12 to 15 minutes or until puffed and golden brown. Remove from oven, turn onto wire rack covered with tea towel. Carefully remove lining paper, spread evenly with Filling. Holding tea towel with both hands, gently roll roulade.

Filling: Combine salmon, shallots, mayonnaise and chives, mix well.

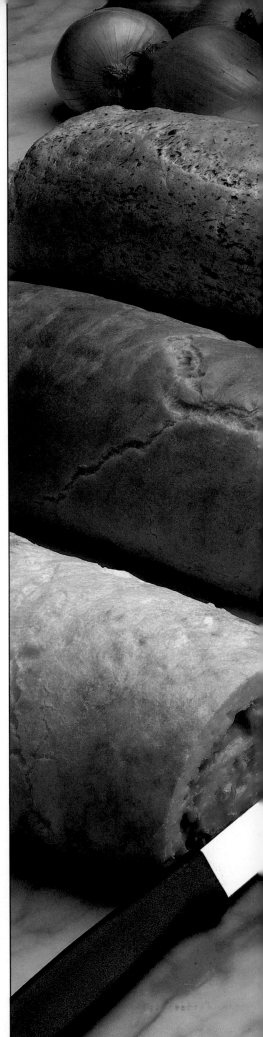

CHEESE AND CORN ROULADE

2 oz butter
⅓ cup all-purpose flour
1 cup milk
4 eggs, separated
¾ cup grated cheddar cheese
FILLING
1 bacon slice, chopped
10-oz can creamed corn
1 teaspoon cornstarch
2 teaspoons water
2 tablespoons sour cream
1 tablespoon chopped chives

Melt butter in pan, add flour, stir 1 minute. Add milk gradually, stir until mixture boils and thickens. Quickly stir in egg yolks and cheese; transfer mixture to large bowl. Beat egg whites until soft peaks form, fold lightly into cheese mixture. Pour mixture into greased, greaseproof paper–lined 10x12-inch Swiss roll pan. Bake in hot oven 12 to 15 minutes or until puffed and golden brown. Remove from oven, turn onto wire rack covered with dish towel. Carefully remove lining paper. Spread evenly with Filling. Holding dish towel with both hands, gently roll roulade.
Filling: Fry bacon until golden and crisp, add corn and blended cornstarch and water. Stir until mixture boils and thickens. Stir in sour cream and chives.

TOMATO AND ZUCCHINI ROULADE

2 oz butter
½ cup all-purpose flour
1 cup milk
4 eggs, separated
2 tablespoons tomato paste
FILLING
12 oz zucchini, grated
salt
1 onion, chopped
1 oz butter
1 teaspoon French mustard
2 teaspoons cornstarch
1 tablespoon sour cream

Melt butter in pan, add flour, stir 1 minute. Add milk gradually, stir until moisture boils and thickens. Quickly stir in egg yolks and tomato paste, transfer mixture to large bowl. Beat egg whites until soft peaks form, fold into tomato mixture. Pour mixture into greased, greaseproof paper–lined 10x12-inch Swiss roll pan. Bake in hot oven 12 to 15 minutes or until puffed and golden brown. Remove from oven, turn onto wire rack covered with tea towel. Carefully remove lining paper. Spread evenly with Filling. Holding tea towel with both hands, gently roll roulade.
Filling: Sprinkle zucchini with salt, stand 1 hour. Rinse zucchini under cold running water, drain well. Squeeze out excess moisture with hands. Sauté onion in butter until tender, add mustard and zucchini, cook 1 minute. Add blended cornstarch and sour cream, stir until mixture boils and thickens.

Flans

Flans are best eaten warm, so prepare the pastry and the filling up to a day before required, then fill the pastry case and bake on the day of serving. The flans should stand about 15 minutes before cutting.

SPINACH AND COTTAGE CHEESE FLAN
8 leaves filo dough
2 oz butter, melted
1 lb cottage cheese
½ x ½-pint carton sour cream
3 eggs
3 bacon slices, chopped
1 onion, chopped
8 spinach leaves, chopped
2 tablespoons all-purpose flour
2 tomatoes, slice
¼ cup grated Parmesan cheese
1 teaspoon dried basil leaves

Layer sheets of pastry, brushing between each sheet with butter. Lift pastry into 10-inch flan tin, press over base and side. Trim pastry edge to about ¾ inches higher than side of tin.

Blend or process cottage cheese, sour cream and eggs until smooth. Fry bacon until lightly browned, add onion, cook until onion is tender. Add spinach, cook until just wilted, remove from heat. Mix in flour and cottage cheese mixture. Pour into pastry case.

Place tomatoes around edge of flan. Sprinkle with combined Parmesan cheese and basil. Bake in moderately hot oven 15 minutes, reduce to moderate, bake further 20 to 30 minutes.

TASTY POTATO FLAN
PASTRY
1 cup all-purpose flour
½ cup grated cheddar cheese
1 egg yolk
2 tablespoons milk, approximately
TOPPING
2 cups mashed potato
2 oz butter, melted
¼ cup mile
2 tablespoons mayonnaise
1 egg
3 bacon slices, chopped
2 shallots, chopped
10-oz can creamed corn
½ cup grated cheese

Pastry: Sift flour into bowl, rub in butter, mix in cheese, egg yolk and enough milk to mix to firm dough. Roll out large enough to line 10-inch flan tin, prick base well. Bake in moderately hot oven 10 minutes.

Topping: Combine potato, butter, milk, mayonnaise and egg, mix well, spread half over pastry case. Cook bacon until crisp, drain, mix in shallots and corn, spread over potato mixture, top with remaining potato mixture, sprinkle with grated cheese and bake in moderate oven for 30 minutes.

LEEK AND WATERCRESS FLAN
PASTRY
1½ cups all-purpose flour
3 oz butter
2 egg yolks
2 tablespoons water, approximately
FILLING
3 leeks, finely sliced
1 clove garlic, crushed
2 oz butter
2 cups watercress, firmly packed
8-oz packet cream cheese
2 eggs
¾ cup grated cheddar cheese
1 tablespoon lemon juice
2 tablespoons chopped walnuts

Pastry: Sift flour into bowl, rub in butter, add egg yolks and enough water to mix to a firm dough. Roll out pastry large enough to line 10-inch flan tin, trim edges. Cover pastry in flan pan with greaseproof paper, then fill with dried beans or rice. Bake in moderate oven 10 minutes, remove beans and paper. Return flan to oven, bake further 7 minutes, cool. Spoon in Filling, sprinkle with walnuts, bake in moderate oven 25 minutes or until Filling is set.

Filling: Sauté leeks and garlic in butter, cover, cook over low heat 15 minutes. Add watercress, cook 1 minute. Beat cream cheese until softened, stir in eggs, cheese, lemon juice and leek mixture.

Back: Tasty Potato Flan.
Top left: Spinach and Cottage Cheese Flan.
Center right: Leek and Watercress Flan.

Sausages

Use thin sausages for quick cooking and easier eating. If your guests have to stand while eating, cut the sausages into manageable pieces. Both of these dishes will give about 10 small servings when accompanied by other dishes.

TOMATO SAUSAGES WITH CORNMEAL TOPPING

2¼ lb thin sausages
1 tablespoon oil
2 onions, sliced
2 tomatoes, chopped
4 oz tomato soup
¼ cup water

CORNMEAL TOPPING

¾ cup self-rising flour
2 teaspoons sugar
⅓ cup cornmeal
1 tablespoon chopped parsley
1 egg
½ cup milk
1½ tablespoons oil

Heat oil in pan, add sausages, cook until golden brown all over. Remove from pan, place in ovenproof dish in single layer. Drain away excess oil from pan, add onion, cook until transparent. Add tomatoes, undiluted soup and water, stir until mixture boils, simmer uncovered 5 minutes, pour over sausages. Spread Cornmeal Topping evenly over tomato mixture to cover completely. Bake in moderate oven 30 minutes or until golden brown.

Cornmeal Topping: Combine sifted flour with sugar, cornmeal and parsley in bowl, stir in combined egg, milk and oil, mix well.

BAKED BEAN AND SAUSAGE CASSEROLE

3¼ lb thin sausages
2 tablespoons oil
2 onions, sliced
2 teaspoons curry powder
15-oz can baked beans
15-oz can Italian Cooking Sauce
1 tablespoon soy sauce
1 teaspoon Worcestershire sauce

Prick sausages well with skewer, place in large pan, cover with water, bring to boil, cover, reduce heat, simmer 10 minutes, drain. Remove skins from sausages, cut sausages in half.

Heat oil in pan, cook onions and curry powder until onions are tender. Add baked beans, Italian Cooking Sauce, soy sauce and Worcestershire sauce, bring to boil, simmer 15 minutes.

Croissant Fillings

Croissants can be bought fresh from bakeries or frozen in packages. The Fillings given at right are sufficient to fill six croissants.

Waffle Toppings

Toast frozen waffles, butter them if you like, give people a choice of toppings.

HAM AND PINEAPPLE WAFFLES
6 frozen waffles
6 slices ham, chopped
3 slices canned pineapple, chopped
½ cup grated mozzarella cheese
Toast waffles as directed on packet, top with ham and pineapple. Sprinkle with mozzarella cheese. Grill until cheese is melted and slightly browned and serve immediately.

TURKEY AND CRANBERRY WAFFLES
6 frozen waffles
6 slices turkey
1 cup alfalfa sprouts
7 oz cottage cheese
2 tablespoons chopped chives
¾ x 8-oz jar cranberry sauce
¼ cup crabapple jelly
1 tablespoon port
Top toasted waffles with turkey and sprouts, then combined cottage cheese and chives. Combine cranberry sauce, crabapple jelly and port. Stir over low heat until well mixed. Spoon over waffles just before serving.

BACON AND MUSHROOM FILLING

This filling is not suitable for freezing.

2 tablespoons mayonnaise
2 tablespoons sour cream
½ teaspoon French mustard
2 bacon slices, chopped
2 shallots, chopped
2 oz mushrooms, chopped

Combine mayonnaise with sour cream and mustard. Cook bacon until crisp. Spread mayonnaise mixture over one half of each croissant. Sprinkle with bacon and shallots, top with mushrooms, then other half of croissant. Bake uncovered in moderate oven for about 10 minutes.

CHICKEN, ALMOND AND BACON FILLING

This filling can be placed into split frozen croissants, refrozen, then heated uncovered in moderate oven for 15 to 20 minutes.

¼ cooked chicken
1 bacon slice, chopped
2 tablespoons slivered almonds
1 tablespoon chopped chives
½ cup sour cream

Toast almonds in moderate oven 8 minutes. Remove chicken meat from bones, chop chicken finely. Cook bacon in pan until crisp, drain. Combine chicken, bacon, almonds, chives and sour cream. Fill croissants and heat in moderate oven for 10 minutes.

CREAM CHEESE AND CHIVE FILLING

8-oz packet cream cheese
1 oz butter
1 teaspoon mustard
1 teaspoon grated lemon rind
1 tablespoon lemon juice
¼ cup chopped chives

Heat croissants in moderate oven. Beat cheese, butter, mustard and lemon rind and juice until soft and creamy. Stir in chives. Spread into hot croissants.

Breads, etc.

Muffins are quick and easy to make. They freeze well for up to a month if you don't have time to cook at the last minute. Wrap the cold muffins in a single layer of aluminum foil, freeze. Thaw frozen in foil in moderate oven for 20 to 30 minutes. We used deep muffin tins of ⅓-cup fluid capacity for our recipes. Serve muffins hot with butter—they're irresistible.

CARROT AND ZUCCHINI MUFFINS
2 cups self-rising flour
½ cup brown sugar, firmly packed
½ teaspoon baking soda
1 teaspoon cinnamon
1 cup grated carrot, lightly packed
1 cup grated zucchini, lightly packed
½ cup chopped walnuts
2 eggs
¾ cup milk
3 oz butter, melted

Sift flour, sugar, soda and cinnamon into a bowl, mix in carrot, zucchini and walnuts. Make well in center of dry ingredients, add lightly beaten eggs, milk and butter, mix with fork until ingredients are just combined. Drop tablespoonfuls of mixture into greased muffin tins, bake in moderately hot oven 20 minutes.
   Makes 12.

BANANA PECAN MUFFINS
1½ cups whole-wheat flour
½ teaspoon baking powder
1 teaspoon baking soda
1½ cups unprocessed bran
¾ cup raw sugar
½ cup chopped pecans or walnuts
2 large very ripe bananas, mashed
4 oz butter, melted
1 egg
1 cup buttermilk

Sift flour, baking powder and soda into bowl, return husks from sifter to bowl. Mix in bran, sugar and pecans. Make well in center of dry ingredients, add bananas, butter, lightly beaten egg and buttermilk, mix with fork only until combined. Fill greased muffin tins, bake in moderately hot oven 25 to 27 minutes or until toothpick inserted in center comes out clean.
   Makes 12.

SPIRAL HERB BREAD

This bread is at its best made on the day it is to be eaten.

¾ cup milk
2 oz butter
1 tablespoon sugar
1 teaspoon salt
¼ oz sachet dry yeast
1 egg
3 cups all-purpose flour
1 egg, extra
melted butter
HERB FILLING
½ oz butter
½ cup chopped parsley
½ cup chopped shallots
⅓ cup chopped chives

Combine milk, butter, sugar and salt in pan, stir until milk is lukewarm. Remove from heat, stir until butter is melted. Add yeast, stir until dissolved; transfer to bowl. Stir lightly beaten egg and flour into liquid, mix to a firm dough. Knead dough on lightly floured surface for about 5 minutes, or until smooth and elastic. Return dough to bowl, cover, stand in warm place 1½ hours until dough is doubled in bulk. Punch dough down, turn onto floured surface, knead until dough is smooth and elastic. Roll dough out to 8x16-inch rectangle. Brush dough with lightly beaten extra egg. Add any remaining beaten egg to Herb Filling. Spread Filling evenly over dough. Starting from narrow end, roll dough up like a Swiss roll. Pinch dough together at both ends to cover exposed Filling. Place into greased 4x7-inch loaf pan with joint facing down. Brush top with melted butter. Cover, stand in warm place 1 hour until dough is doubled in bulk. Bake in moderate oven 40 to 50 minutes. Cool on wire rack.

Herb Filling: Melt butter in pan, add parsley, shallots and chives, cook stirring for 30 seconds, remove from heat, cool.

WHOLE-WHEAT CHEESE AND BACON MUFFINS

4 bacon slices, chopped
2 green onions, chopped
1½ cups whole-wheat flour
1 tablespoon baking powder
1 tablespoon sugar
¼ cup bulgur (cracked wheat)
1 oz butter
1 cup grated cheddar cheese
1 egg
¾ cup milk

Fry bacon until crisp, add green onions, drain on paper towel.

Sift flour and sugar into bowl, return husks from sifter to bowl; add bulgur, rub in butter. Mix in half the cheese, make well in center of dry ingredients, add lightly beaten egg and milk. Mix with fork only until ingredients are moistened. Half fill greased muffin tins with mixture, sprinkle with bacon mixture, top with remaining muffin mixture. Top with remaining cheese, bake in moderately hot oven 20 minutes.

Makes 12.

FRESH HERB BISCUITS

Make the biscuits and serve while hot, or freeze like the muffins.

2 cups self-rising flour
1 teaspoon sugar
1 oz butter
¼ chopped chives
¼ cup chopped fresh dill
¼ cup chopped parsley
½ cup milk
⅓ cup water, approximately

Sift flour and sugar into bowl, rub in butter. Stir in chives, dill and parsley. Pour in milk and enough water to mix to a sticky dough. Turn onto lightly floured surface, knead lightly until smooth. Pat dough out to approximately ¾-inch thickness; cut into rounds with 2-inch cutter. Place biscuits in a lightly greased 8-inch round sandwich tin. Brush tops with a little milk. Bake in very hot oven 15 to 20 minutes or until golden brown.

Makes 12.

WHOLEMEAL DAMPER

1 cup whole-wheat flour
2 cups self-rising flour
2 teaspoons baking powder
¼ teaspoon salt
2 teaspoons sugar
½ cup milk
¾ cup water, approximately

Sift flours, salt, baking powder and sugar into bowl, make well in center, pour in milk and most of the water, all at once. Mix with a knife to a moist, sticky dough. Add more water if necessary. Turn onto lightly floured surface, knead into round shape; place on greased tray. Pat dough out to 6-inch circle. With sharp knife, cut 2 slits about ¼ inch deep across dough like a cross; do not cut right to edge. Brush top with milk or water, sift a little extra flour over top of damper. Bake in very hot oven 10 minutes, reduce to moderate, bake further 20 to 30 minutes, or until golden brown.

Muffin Toppings

English muffins are available in many varieties. Split and toast them, then choose from our Toppings. There are enough ingredients for six muffins.

PEANUT, BANANA AND BACON TOPPING
crunchy peanut butter
4 bananas, sliced
¼ cup lemon juice
12 slices bacon
Spread muffin halves with peanut butter. Top with banana dipped in lemon juice. Remove rind from bacon, cut in half, grill until almost crisp, place over bananas. Continue to grill until the bacon is crisp and brown.

AVOCADO AND BLUE CHEESE TOPPING
mayonnaise
1 small lettuce, coarsely shredded
2 avocados, sliced
8 oz blue vein cheese
Butter muffin halves, spread with mayonnaise, top with lettuce, avocado and slices of cheese.

PIZZA-STYLE TOPPING
tomato paste
12 slices salami
4 slices mozzarella cheese
stuffed green olives
Spread tomato paste lightly over muffin halves; top each with a slice of salami, then strips of mozzarella, top with sliced olives. Grill until cheese is melted.

Fritters

Fritters are a last-minute cooking job. Set up an electric frying pan or two, supply the ready-made mixtures and the necessary equipment, and let your guests make their own.

CRISPY POTATO FRITTERS
2 large potatoes
2 bacon slices, chopped
1 tablespoon self-rising flour
oil
Peel and coarsely grate potatoes, rinse potato strips under cold running water until water is clear, drain and pat dry. Combine potato strips with bacon and flour, toss lightly with fork until well combined. Heat pan, add about 2 tablespoons oil. When oil is hot, add tablespoons of potato mixture to pan, spread mixture out to thin rounds. Fry until golden brown on both sides. Drain on kitchen paper.
	Makes approximately 20.

Jams

Turn an inexpensive jam or marmalade into something special by adding a few ingredients. Try the Honey Orange Butter on toast, biscuits or muffins –- it's delicious.

LIME AND GINGER JAM
1-lb jar lime marmalade
3 teaspoons grated fresh ginger
2 oz glace ginger
Place jam in pan. Squeeze grated ginger between 2 teaspoons to extract juice, add to jam. Slice glace ginger thinly, then cut into fine strips; add to jam.

Stir over low heat until ingredients are combined; cool.

ALMOND STRAWBERRY JAM
1 lb strawberry jam
2 tablespoons Kirsch
2 tablespoons slivered almonds
Place almonds on flat tray, bake in moderate oven 8 minutes or until light golden brown.

Combine jam and Kirsch in pan, stir over low heat until combined, gently stir in almonds; cool.

ORANGE MARNIER MARMALADE
1½ x 1-lb cans orange marmalade
2 tablespoons Grand Marnier
pinch cinnamon
Stir marmalade in pan over very low heat until beginning to soften. Stir in Grand Marnier and cinnamon; cool.

HONEY ORANGE BUTTER
½ lb butter
1 teaspoon grated orange rind
2 tablespoons orange juice
½ cup honey
¼ teaspoon cinnamon
Beat butter until creamy in electric mixer. Beat in orange rind and juice, then honey and cinnamon.

CRUNCHY CORN FRITTERS

We used 2 cobs of corn to get 2 cups of kernels required for this recipe; the fresh flavor is worth the little extra trouble.

1 cup all-purpose flour
2 eggs
½ cup milk
½ cup cream
2 cups fresh corn kernels
½ cup chopped shallots
½ cup grated cheddar cheese
oil
Sift flour into bowl, stir in combined eggs, milk and cream, beat until smooth, stir in corn, shallots and cheese. Heat about 2 tablespoons oil in pan, drop tablespoons of corn mixture into pan, spread mixture out slightly. Fry until golden brown on both sides.

Makes about 30.

Champagne and Chicken Lunch

Chicken and champagne always sounds celebratory. This menu is glamorous and tastes wonderful. Serve with well-chilled champagne, or try one of our Champagne Cocktails on page 123. The recipes will serve ten people.

CHICKEN WITH SWEET CURRIED MAYONNAISE

Prepare the Mayonnaise the day before required. The chicken is best cooked in the morning up to several hours before lunch.

10 chicken breast fillets
4 oz butter, melted
1 tablespoon lemon juice
SWEET CURRIED MAYONNAISE
1 tablespoon oil
1 onion, finely chopped
2 teaspoons curry powder
2 tablespoons tomato sauce
2 tablespoons dry white wine
2 tablespoons apricot jam
11-oz jar mayonnaise

Choose ovenproof dish large enough to hold chicken fillets in single layer. Melt butter and lemon juice in dish, add chicken fillets, coat all over with butter. Cover with greaseproof paper, then aluminum foil, prick holes in foil in a few places. Bake in moderate oven 15 minutes or until chicken is tender. Remove chicken, pat dry on kitchen paper, arrange on serving dish, cover with greaseproof paper, refrigerate while preparing Mayonnaise.

Sweet Curried Mayonnaise: Heat oil in pan, add onion, cook until transparent, add curry powder, cook 2 minutes. Add tomato sauce and wine, simmer uncovered until reduced by half. Add jam, stir until melted, cool, strain, then stir into mayonnaise. Coat chicken with Mayonnaise up to an hour before serving.

LOBSTER AND AVOCADO SALAD

Prepare lobster and Dressing the day before required. Avocados must be sliced as close to serving time as possible. Brush with Dressing to prevent discoloration.

3 cooked lobsters
3 avocados
4 heads butter lettuce
DRESSING
⅓ cup oil
2 tablespoons lemon juice
1½ teaspoons sugar
1 tablespoon canned green peppercorns
1 teaspoon grated fresh ginger

Remove lobster tails from shell, slice crossways. Peel and seed avocados, slice thinly. Arrange lobster and avocado on bed of lettuce, pour Dressing over.
Dressing: Combine all ingredients.

GRILLED PEPPER AND CAVIAR SALAD

Prepare peppers and celery up to a day ahead, store covered in refrigerator. Toss salad up to an hour before serving.

6 green bell peppers
6 red bell peppers
4 sticks celery
2-oz jar black caviar
DRESSING
⅓ cup oil
1½ tablespoons white vinegar
1 tablespoon capers

Cut peppers in half, broil, cut side down until skin blisters and blackens; cool. Peel away skin, cut peppers into think strips about 2 inches long, cut celery the same length as peppers. Combine peppers and celery with Dressing. Toss lightly, garnish with caviar.
Dressing: Combine all ingredients.

POTATO SALAD WITH GREEN PEA MAYONNAISE

Cook potatoes and prepare the mayonnaise the day before serving. Combine the two up to an hour before lunch.

2¼ lb baby white potatoes
1 cup frozen peas
½ cup sour cream
½ cup mayonnaise
2 cloves garlic, crushed
2 tablespoons chopped mint
2 tablespoons chopped chives

Boil or steam potatoes until just tender, drain, refresh under cold water, drain, refrigerate until ready to mix with the mayonnaise. Add peas to boiling water, cook 5 minutes, drain, refresh under cold water until completely cold, drain. Puree or process peas with sour cream, mayonnaise, garlic, mint and chives until smooth, spoon over potatoes.

CHOCOLATE ALMOND RUM CAKE

This cake is rich and moist. Serve in slim wedges with or without whipped cream.

8 oz dark cooking chocolate
⅓ cup rum
8 oz unsalted butter
1 cup sugar
6 eggs, separated
2 tablespoons sugar, extra
1 cup ground almonds
¾ cup all-purpose flour
CHOCOLATE ICING
4 oz dark cooking chocolate
4 oz unsalted butter
2 tablespoons rum
1 cup flaked almonds

Melt chocolate and rum over hot water; cool, do not allow to set. Cream butter and sugar until light and fluffy, add egg yolks gradually, beat well. Transfer mixture to a large bowl, stir in chocolate mixture and almonds. Beat egg whites until firm peaks from, add extra sugar, beat until dissolved. Fold egg whites and sifted flour into chocolate mixture in several batches. Spread into well-greased, deep 10-inch round cake pan that has base lined with greased greaseproof paper. Bake in moderate oven 50 minutes. Stand 5 minutes before turning onto wire rack to cool. When cold, spread top and side with Chocolate Icing, press toasted flaked almonds around side (spread almonds on flat oven tray, bake in moderate oven 5 minutes, cool). Decorate with crystallized violets.

Chocolate Icing: Melt chocolate, butter and rum together over hot water, stir until smooth, cool until thick and spreadable before using.

Crystallized Violets: Choose fresh violets. Use small paintbrush to brush egg white evenly but sparingly over both sides of violets. Make sure to brush where petals overlap. Sprinkle evenly with colored fine granulated sugar, gently shake off excess sugar. Stand violets on wire rack, leave in warm dry place until dry; time will depend on weather. Drying can be hurried by placing rack of violets on door of opened oven, with oven on a slow temperature.

To color sugar: Place sugar in plastic bag, add a drop or two of purple food coloring, rub coloring through sugar by rubbing outside of plastic bag. This method saves colored fingers.

Store dry violets in airtight container with tissue paper between them. Violets are edible.

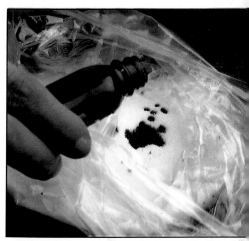

Vegetarian Lunch

Serve a vegetarian lunch and wait for the compliments. The food is tasty, filling and nutritious. Serve some wholemeal bread or rolls with the meal. The food will serve six.

PUMPKIN FLANS

Flan cases can be made up to a week in advance and stored in an airtight container. Use leftover pumpkin, providing it has not been mashed with milk, butter, cream, etc.

WHOLE-WHEAT PASTRY
1 cup whole-wheat flour
1 cup all-purpose flour
2 teaspoons baking powder
pinch nutmeg
4 oz butter
⅓ cup cold water, approximately
FILLING
1½ cups cold mashed pumpkin
½ small onion, chopped
1 clove garlic, crushed
2 eggs
½ x ½ pint thickened cream
¼ cup grated Parmesan cheese
2 shallots, chopped
paprika

Pastry: Sift flour and nutmeg into bowl, rub in butter, add enough water to mix to a firm dough. Roll out large enough to line 6 individual 4½-inch flan pans. Cover pastry with greaseproof paper, sprinkle thickly with rice or beans and bake in moderately hot oven for 10 minutes. Remove paper and beans, return cases to oven for 7 to 10 minutes. Add Filling, bake for 20 minutes or until knife inserted in center comes out clean.

Filling: Blend or process pumpkin, onion and garlic until smooth. Add eggs, cream and cheese. Pour into flan cases, sprinkle with shallots and paprika.

SPAGHETTI WITH TOMATO AND MINT SAUCE

We have included anchovy fillets in this recipe as a flavor booster; omit if desired.

2 tablespoons pine nuts
10 oz butter
½ x 1½-oz can anchovy fillets, chopped
2 onions, chopped
4 ripe tomatoes, peeled and chopped
1 tablespoon tomato paste
¼ cup water
8 oz spaghetti
2 tablespoons chopped mint

Brown pine nuts in pan over low heat; cool. Melt butter in pan, add drained anchovy fillets and onion, stir until onion is transparent Stir in tomatoes and tomato paste, cook 1 minute. Add water, reduce heat and simmer gently, uncovered, for 15 minutes.

Cook spaghetti in boiling water 10 minutes or until just tender, drain. Spoon tomato mixture over spaghetti, serve sprinkled with mint and pine nuts. Serve with Parmesan cheese, if desired.

OLIVE NUT LOAF

Make this bread as close to serving time as possible for best results and serve it hot with butter. It can be made up to a month in advance, cooled and frozen, wrapped in foil; then thaw in moderate oven for about 30 minutes.

3 oz butter, melted
1 onion, finely chopped
½ cup chopped pecan nuts
½ cup chopped blanched almonds
½ cup chopped black olives
1½ cups buttermilk
2 eggs
1 cup self-rising flour
½ cup all-purpose flour
1 cup whole-wheat flour
1 teaspoon baking soda

Saute onion in butter until transparent, add nuts, stir constantly over low heat 3 minutes, remove from heat. Combine olives, buttermilk and eggs in bowl, beat with fork until combined. Sift flours and soda into bowl, add nut and buttermilk mixture, mix until well combined. Spoon mixture into greased 4½x7-inch loaf pan. Bake in moderate oven 50 minutes.

BEAN SALAD

1 lettuce
1 cup mung bean sprouts
¾ x 14-oz can red kidney beans
½ x 10-oz can butter beans
  (cannellini style)
4 shallots, chopped
½ bunch radishes, sliced
DRESSING
2 ripe tomatoes, peeled
½ small onion
1 small clove garlic, crushed
⅓ cup oil
1 tablespoon lemon juice
2 teaspoons honey
1½ cups fresh basil leaves
1 cup fresh parsley sprigs

Line salad bowl with lettuce leaves. Toss together sprouts, drained and rinsed beans, shallots and radishes; place in salad bowl. Serve Dressing separately.
Dressing: Puree or process all ingredients until smooth.

RICOTTA BUTTERMILK CHEESECAKE

Make the cheesecake the day before needed, keep covered and refrigerated. The texture is smooth and the flavor delicate. Use any berries, fresh or frozen, sweetened to your taste, for a sauce. Check your springform pan for leaks by filling with water. If it leaks, wrap outside of pan in aluminum foil before placing in baking dish with water.

1½ lb ricotta cheese
4 eggs
1 cup buttermilk
½ cup honey
2 teaspoons grated lemon rind
2 teaspoons lemon juice
STRAWBERRY SAUCE
½ lb strawberries
½ cup powdered sugar
2 teaspoons lemon juice

Beat ricotta cheese in electric mixer, add eggs, one at a time, beating well after each addition. Add buttermilk, honey, lemon rind and juice; beat until combined. Pour mixture into greased 8-inch springform pan. Bake, standing in dish with hot water coming halfway up sides, in moderate oven for 1 hour or until top feels firm. Allow to come to room temperature before removing from tin. Serve with Strawberry Sauce.
Strawberry Sauce: Puree or process strawberries with sifted powdered sugar and lemon juice, strain.

Dieters' Lunch for 8

Surprise your friends by serving them a delightful low-calorie lunch. The Eggplant Parmigiana can be served as an entrée or with the Fish Parcels so that you have a choice of main courses. Calorie count for the lunch is about 425 per person. (This doesn't include the fruit.)

EGGPLANT PARMIGIANA

Prepare up to 24 hours before baking.

1 lb eggplant (about 2 small eggplants)
1½ cups chicken stock
14½-oz can tomatoes
1 chicken stock cube
1 onion, chopped
1 clove garlic, crushed
4 oz mushrooms, sliced
1 tablespoon tomato paste
1 tablespoon chopped parsley
2 tablespoons grated Parmesan cheese
SAUCE
1 oz butter
2 tablespoons all-purpose flour
1½ cups skim milk
½ teaspoon dry mustard
1 egg

Cut unpeeled eggplant into dice. Bring stock to boil, add eggplant, boil 1 minute; drain. Pour undrained tomatoes into pan, add crumbled stock cube, onion and garlic, bring to boil, reduce heat, simmer uncovered 10 minutes. Stir in mushrooms, tomato paste and parsley, cook further 1 minute. Divide mixture into 8 individual heatproof dishes of ½ cup capacity. Spoon Sauce over top, sprinkle with cheese. Bake in moderate oven 15 minutes or until golden brown.

Sauce: Melt butter in pan, add flour and stir over heat for 1 minute. Add milk and mustard, bring to boil, stirring until Sauce thickens. Remove from heat, stir in egg.

Approximately 100 calories per serving.

WILD RICE SALAD

Combine cooked rice and vegetables up to 24 hours before serving, cover, refrigerate. Add almonds and Dressing just before serving.

6½ oz wild rice
⅓ cup long-grain rice
2 tablespoons flaked almonds
1 red bell pepper
2 zucchini
4 shallots
DRESSING
2 tablespoons light sour cream
1 tablespoon oil
2 tablespoons lemon juice

Cook wild rice according to directions on package (see note below). Add rice to large quantity of boiling water. Boil rapidly uncovered 10 minutes, drain. Toast almonds on flat tray in moderate oven 5 to 10 minutes. Cut red bell pepper, zucchini and shallots into thin strips 1 inch in length. Combine all ingredients, toss with Dressing.

Dressing: Combine all ingredients in screw-top jar, shake well.

Approximately 120 calories per serving.

Note: If wild rice is too crunchy for your taste, after following package instructions, boil in large quantity of water for 20 to 30 minutes or until as tender as desired.

FISH PARCELS WITH JULIENNE VEGETABLES

Prepare fish parcels several hours before cooking.

1 carrot
2 sticks celery
8 large lettuce leaves
8 whitefish fillets
1 teaspoon dried tarragon
    leaves
2 teaspoons cornstarch
1 tablespoon water
STOCK
1½ cups water
⅓ cup dry white wine
2 sprigs parsley
1 stick celery
1 chicken stock cube

Cut carrot and celery into very thin strips about 2 inches long. Drop lettuce leaves into large pan of boiling water one by one, boil for 30 seconds each, or until they are just wilted and bright green. Drain on kitchen paper. Remove skin and bones from fish, sprinkle evenly with tarragon. Place 1 piece of fish on each lettuce leaf, fold in both sides of leaf, roll up into a parcel. Repeat with remaining fish and lettuce leaves. Place parcels in pan in single layer. Pour stock over, cover, bring to boil, reduce heat, simmer covered 6 minutes or until fish is tender. Place on serving dish, keep warm. Add carrot and celery to stock, bring to boil. Stir in blended cornstarch and water, stir until sauce boils and thickens. Spoon sauce over fish parcels.

Stock: Combine water, wine, parsley, celery and crumbled stock cube in pan, bring to boil, reduce heat, simmer covered 10 minutes, strain.

Approximately 160 calories per serving.

76

YOGURT CREAM TOPPING

Use a thick yogurt (not the low-fat type) for best results.

2 x 6-oz cartons plain yogurt
3 tablespoons whipping cream

Stir ingredients together until smooth, cover, refrigerate overnight. Serve with a selection of fresh fruit.

Approximately 65 calories per serving.

Here are a dozen delightful new desserts to provide a grand finale to your entertaining. Most of them can be prepared, in whole or in part, up to a week before they are needed. Some will keep for a month. But the delicate Liqueur Fruits with Mango Cream is a last-minute effort. Be guided by notes at the head of each recipe.

LEMON CREAM CHEESE BUTTER CAKE

Cake will freeze well for up to a month. Top with glaze several hours before serving. We like this cake served plain, or with whipped cream as a dessert.

4-oz package cream cheese
8 oz butter
2 teaspoons grated lemon rind
1½ cups sugar
3 eggs
1½ cups all-purpose flour
LEMON GLAZE
1 cup powdered sugar
2 teaspoons lemon juice,
  approximately

Beat cream cheese, butter and lemon rind together until smooth, add sugar, beat until light and fluffy. Beat in eggs one at a time, stir in sifted flour in two batches, beat lightly until smooth. Spoon into well-greased 8-inch ring or baba tin. Bake in moderate oven 30 minutes, reduce temperature to moderately slow, bake further 30 minutes. Cool in tin 10 minutes, turn onto wire rack. When cold, top with Lemon Glaze
Lemon Glaze: Sift powdered sugar into bowl, beat in enough lemon juice to give a pouring consistency.

77

LIQUEUR FRUITS WITH MANGO CREAM

Prepare this delicate dish as close to serving time as possible. Choose any combination of fruits.

2 mangoes
2 kiwifruit
½ lb raspberries (or any other berries)
⅓ cup Grand Marnier
2 passion fruit
MANGO CREAM
1 mango
¾ cup thickened cream

Peel mangoes, cut pulp from stone, then cut pulp into thick strips. Peel kiwifruit, cut into thick slices. Place raspberries, mango and kiwifruit in 6 individual serving dishes. Sprinkle Grand Marnier over fruit, refrigerate until ready to serve.

Top fruit with Mango Cream and passion fruit.

Mango Cream: Puree, process or blend mango pulp until smooth. Beat cream until firm peaks form, fold in mango puree.

Serves 6.

CARAMEL CRUNCH CHEESECAKE

This is a super-rich cheesecake. It can be made and refrigerated for up to two days before required and freezes well for up to a month. Cut in slender wedges, it would serve about 10 people.

BASE
4 oz plain chocolate cookies, finely crushed
2 oz butter, melted
1 teaspoon water
FILLING
2 x 8-oz packets cream cheese
⅓ cup sugar
2 teaspoons grated lemon rind
3 eggs
⅓ cup cream
1 tablespoon all-purpose flour
1 oz butter
¼ cup brown sugar
2 tablespoons hot water
condensed milk
1½-oz bar chocolate-coated honeycomb, finely chopped
TOPPING
4½ oz dark cooking chocolate
¼ cup cream

Base: Combine cookies, butter and water, mix well, press evenly over base of 8-inch springform pan; refrigerate 30 minutes.

Filling: Beat cream cheese until soft, beat in sugar and lemon rind, then eggs one at a time, then cream and flour. Combine butter, sugar, condensed milk, golden syrup and water in pan, stir over heat until sugar is dissolved. Bring to boil, boil rapidly without stirring for about 4 minutes or until deep caramel color. Cool for 10 minutes.

Pour half the cream cheese mixture over crumb base. Sprinkle with honeycomb bar, spoon caramel evenly over honeycomb, then top with remaining cream cheese mixture. Bake in slow oven 1 hour, cool to room temperature. Spread Topping over cheesecake, refrigerate until set.

Topping: Melt chocolate with cream in pan over low heat; do not boil.

PECAN PRALINE CHEESECAKE

You will need about 6 ounces pecans for this recipe; reserve about 12 for decoration. This cheese cake is rich. Cut in slender wedges, it should serve about 12 people.

CRUMB CRUST
4 oz wheat-wheat cookies, crushed (about 16)
2 oz butter, melted
FILLING
3 x 8-oz cartons cream cheese
2 teaspoons vanilla
1¼ cups brown sugar, firmly packed
3 eggs
2 tablespoons all-purpose flour
1 cup finely chopped pecans
TOPPING
½ cup brown sugar, firmly packed
2 oz butter
½ pint cream
12 pecans
PECAN PRALINE
½ cup sugar
2 tablespoons water
½ cup pecans

Crumb Crust: Combine crumbs and butter in bowl, mix well. Press over base of 9-inch springform pan, refrigerate 30 minutes. Pour Filling into Crumb Crust, bake in moderate oven 50 minutes or until it is set, cool, cover, refrigerate overnight. Remove from springform pan, place onto serving plate. Pour hot Topping over cold cake, spread to edges. When Topping is cold, decorate with whipped cream and 12 pecans. Sprinkle with Pecan Praline.

Filling: Beat cream cheese and vanilla until smooth, add brown sugar, beat until smooth, beat in eggs one at a time, then flour. Stir in pecans.

Topping: Combine brown sugar and butter in pan; stir over low heat without boiling for about 5 minutes or until smooth and thick; use while hot.

Pecan Praline: Combine sugar and water in pan, stir over low heat until sugar is dissolved, boil rapidly without stirring until mixture turns light golden brown, about 5 minutes. Add pecans, pour onto greased oven tray. When set, chop as finely as desired. Store any excess Praline in an airtight jar for future use.

STRAWBERRY SHORTCAKE

The Shortcake base can be cooked up to a week before required, cooled and stored in airtight container. Top with strawberries and glaze a day before serving.

½ lb butter
2 teaspoons vanilla
⅓ cup sugar
⅓ cup rice flour
1 cup self-rising flour
1⅓ cups all-purpose flour
TOPPING
½ lb strawberries
½ cup bottled red currant jelly
1 tablespoon brandy

Cream butter, vanilla and sugar until soft and creamy, stir in sifted flours in two batches. Press ingredients together with floured hands. Knead lightly on floured surface until smooth. Press dough evenly over base of greased 9½-inch recess pan, smooth with knife until level. Bake in moderate oven 25 minutes or until light golden brown; cool in tin, place on serving plate. Arrange halved strawberries on top, spoon glaze over, refrigerate 1 hour or until set. Serve with whipped cream.
Topping: Halve strawberries, place red currant jelly in pan, stir over low heat until melted, do not boil; add brandy; spoon glaze over strawberries while still hot.

ALMOND PEAR FLAN

Prepare pastry case up to a day before adding Filling and pears. Bake up to 3 hours before serving.

PASTRY
1¼ cups all-purpose flour
3 oz butter
3 tablespoons sugar
2 egg yolks
FILLING
4 oz butter
⅓ cup sugar
2 eggs
1 cup ground almonds
1 tablespoon all-purpose flour
3 pears, peeled, cored, quartered
2 tablespoons apricot jam

Pastry: Combine all ingredients in processor, process until combined. Remove to lightly floured surface, knead into smooth ball, cover, refrigerate 30 minutes. Roll pastry large enough to line a 9-inch flan tin. Spread Filling into pastry case, place pear quarters over Filling, bake in moderate oven 35 minutes or until golden brown. Brush with warmed sieved apricot jam.
Filling: Cream butter and sugar together until just combined, add eggs one at a time, beating well after each addition. Fold in almonds and flour.

PASSION FRUIT SHERBET

Make Sherbet up to a week before required. Keep covered with aluminum foil while in freezer.

12 large passion fruit
1 cup sugar
3 cups water
¼ cup lemon juice

Cut fruit in half over bowl, scoop out pulp. Strain to remove seeds. You will need ¾ cup juice.

Place sugar in pan with 1 cup of the water. Stir until sugar is dissolved. Bring to boil without stirring. Remove from heat, pour into bowl. When completely cold, add passion fruit juice, lemon juice and remaining water. Pour into 8-inch square cake pan, freeze until set. Process or blend mixture until smooth. Return to tin, freeze until set. Serve with fresh fruit.

Serves 6.

LIME AND GIN MOUSSE

Make the mousse the day before required; any longer and the mousse will toughen. We used a tiny drop of green food coloring to tint the mixture slightly; fold coloring through the mixture with the cream.

4 eggs, separated
½ cup sugar
1 teaspoon grated lime rind
2 teaspoons gelatin
⅓ cup lime juice
1 tablespoon gin
1 tablespoon sugar, extra
⅔ cup cream

Beat egg yolks, sugar and lime rind in small bowl of electric mixer until thick and lemon colored. Sprinkle gelatin over combined lime juice and gin, dissolve over hot water, cool to room temperature. Gradually beat gelatin mixture into egg mixture. Transfer mixture to large bowl. Beat cream until soft peaks from, fold lightly into mousse mixture. Beat egg whites until soft peaks form, beat in extra sugar, beat until dissolved. Fold lightly into mousse mixture, in two batches Pour into 6 individual glasses, refrigerate several hours or overnight.

Serves 6.

ORANGE CREAM CARAMEL

Make up to 2 days before required, leave in tin, covered, refrigerated.

¾ **cup sugar**
¼ **cup lemon juice**
½ **cup water**
4 eggs
⅓ **cup sugar, extra**
½ **pint cream**
1½ **cups milk**
2 teaspoons grated orange rind

Combine sugar, lemon juice and water in pan, stir over low heat without boiling until sugar is dissolved. Bring to boil, do not stir. Boil rapidly, uncovered, until syrup turns golden brown, abut 5 minutes. Pour the syrup into 7-inch round cake pan.

Lightly beat eggs and extra sugar together. Heat cream, milk and orange rind until hot, whisk into egg mixture. Strain moisture into tin, place in baking dish with hot water to come halfway up side of tin. Bake in moderately slow oven 45 to 50 minutes or until set. Remove from water, cool, refrigerate overnight. Turn onto serving dish, decorate with cream and orange segments if desired.

Serves 6.

CHOCOLATE COFFEE MOUSSE TORTE

Complete cake up to a day before required; keep refrigerated. We used freeze-dried granulated coffee in this recipe.

CHOCOLATE SPONGE CAKE
3 eggs
1/2 cup sugar
1/4 cup cornstarch
1/4 cup all-purpose flour
1/4 cup self-rising flour
1/4 cup cocoa
1/2 pint whipping cream
SYRUP
2 tablespoons sugar
1/3 cup water
2 tablespoons Kahlua
  or Tia Maria

COFFEE MOUSSE
2 envelopes unflavored gelatin
½ **cup water**
3 tablespoons instant-coffee powder
1 cup whipping cream
5 eggs, separated
¾ **cup granulated sugar**

Chocolate Sponge Cake: Combine flour, baking powder, salt and cocoa; set aside. In large bowl, beat egg yolks, ⅓ cup sugar and vanilla until thick, about 5 minutes. In small bowl, beat egg white with ⅓ cup sugar until stiff peaks form. Sprinkle flour mixture over egg yolks, top with egg whites. Gently fold mixture until thoroughly blended. Pour into a greased and waxed paper–lined 15x10-inch jelly roll pan. Bake in 375° oven 15 to 20 minutes or until top springs back when lightly touched. Meanwhile, sprinkle cloth towel with about ⅓ cup powdered sugar. Turn cake out onto towel; gently remove waxed paper. With serrated knife, trim off crisp edges if desired; let cool.

Split cake in half horizontally. Line 2 baking sheets with foil, place a layer of cake on each, spoon Syrup evenly over cakes, top with an even layer of Coffee Mousse. Refrigerate 1 hour. Lift cakes onto serving plate, assembling into layers. Trim edges to a neat rectangle. Decorate with whipped cream and chocolate curls if desired.

Syrup: Combine sugar, water and liqueur in pan, stir over heat until sugar is dissolved, do not boil. Cool to room temperature.

Coffee Mousse: Sprinkle gelatin over water, place over hot water stirring until dissolved. Add coffee; cool to room temperature. Whip cream until soft peaks form; do not refrigerate while preparing the rest of the Mousse. Beat egg yolks and sugar until thick, about 5 minutes. Beat egg whites until stiff but not dry. Stir coffee mixture into yolk mixture. Gently fold in whipped cream and egg whites. Use immediately before Mousse sets.

ICED COFFEE MOUSSE WITH MOCHA SAUCE

Make and freeze, covered, for up to a week. Sauce can be made up to two days ahead. This recipe is strictly for coffee fans.

⅓ cup water
1 teaspoon gelatin
3 tablespoons instant coffee powder
2 eggs, separated
⅔ cup sugar
½ pint cream
MOCHA SAUCE
¾ cup roasted coffee beans
⅓ cup sugar
1½ oz butter
2 tablespoons rum
1 teaspoon vanilla
½ pint cream
3 oz dark cooking chocolate

Below top: Iced Coffee Mousse with Mocha Sauce; bottom: Chocolate Cherry Ice Cream.

Sprinkle gelatin over water, dissolve over hot water, stir in coffee, cool to room temperature. Beat egg yolks and sugar together in small bowl of electric mixer until thick and lemon colored, stir in gelatin mixture. Whip cream until soft peaks form, fold into coffee mixture. Beat egg whites until soft peaks form, fold into coffee mixture. Pour into lightly oiled mold of 4-cup capacity; cover, freeze overnight. Turn mousse onto serving plate, return to freezer while making Sauce.

Mocha Sauce: Place coffee beans in food processor, crush coarsely (do not grind finely). Place coffee beans in pan with sugar and butter, stir over heat without boiling until sugar is dissolved. Add rum, bring to boil, reduce heat, simmer, stirring constantly until Sauce turns light golden brown, then add cream and vanilla, simmer 3 minutes. Strain, add chopped chocolate, stir until smooth. Serve Sauce warm or cold.

Serves 8.

CHOCOLATE CHERRY ICE CREAM

Make this ice cream up to a week before it is required, freeze, covered with aluminum foil.

½ gal vanilla ice cream
3 oz dark cooking chocolate
½ cup cream
2 tablespoons cocoa
½ cup slivered almonds
2 tablespoons red glacé cherries, chopped
2 tablespoons green glacé cherries, chopped
2 glacé apricots, chopped
2 glacé pineapple rings, chopped
3.2-oz milk chocolate bar with toasted coconut

Heat chocolate and cream over low heat until chocolate is melted, stir in sifted cocoa, cool to room temperature. Whip cream until soft peaks form. Place almonds on oven tray, bake in moderate oven 8 minutes; cool.

Soften ice cream slightly, divide between 3 bowls. Mix glacé fruits into ice cream in 1 bowl. Spoon ice cream into loaf (base measures 4½ inches x 7 inches). Freeze while preparing next layer. Gently fold chocolate cream into second bowl of ice cream. Spoon chocolate ice cream over first layer. Coarsely grate half of candy bar and chop remainder, add to third bowl of ice cream together with toasted almonds. Spoon over chocolate ice cream. Freeze several hours or overnight.

Picnic for 2

Charm a friend with this delightful food. Serve with well-chilled champagne or white wine.

SMOKED SALMON IN VINE LEAVES

Store leftover grape leaves, covered, in refrigerator for up to two weeks. Use fresh or bottled leaves. If using fresh leaves, boil for about three minutes or until tender.

10 vine leaves
1 cup cooked rice
2 slices smoked salmon, chopped
1 tablespoon sour cream
2 teaspoons capers, chopped
1 teaspoon chopped fresh dill

Drop vine leaves into pan of boiling water, boil 1 minute, drain and pat dry on kitchen paper. Combine rice with salmon, sour cream, capers and dill, mix well. Place a tablespoon of salmon mixture into center of each leaf. Fold in ends and sides of leaves, roll up to form a neat parcel.

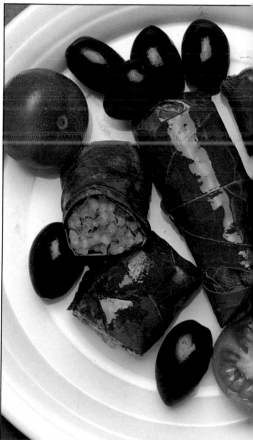

FRUIT CHEESE ROLL

For maximum flavor, prepare the roll at least a day before required; it will keep for up to four days.

½ cup chopped mixed dried fruits
¼ cup chopped mixed glace fruits
2 tablespoons port
8-oz package cream cheese
½ cup grated cheddar cheese
1 teaspoon grated orange rind
¾ cup poppy seeds

Combine fruits in bowl, add port, cover, stand 1 to 2 hours. Beat softened cream cheese and cheddar cheese together in electric mixer, stir in orange rind and fruit mixture; refrigerate, covered, for 1 hour. Roll mixture into log shape about 8 inches in length, roll in poppy seeds, cover, refrigerate 24 hours. Serve with dry cookies.

CHICKEN AND GREEN PEPPERCORN LOAF

Prepare loaf the day before required. Keep covered in refrigerator. Loaf is also delicious eaten hot.

½ lb chicken fillets
2 oz chicken livers
3 bacon slices
1 clove garlic
⅓ cup stale bread crumbs
2 teaspoons canned green peppercorns
2 tablespoons chopped parsley
2 teaspoons brandy
½ x 12-oz packet puff pastry
1 egg white

Grind of process chicken, chicken livers, bacon and garlic. Stir in bread crumbs, peppercorns, parsley and brandy.

Roll out pastry on floured surface, trim to a 12-inch circle. Place chicken mixture in center of pastry, pat into round shape, brush chicken with egg white. Join edges of pastry at top with egg white. Turn loaf over and place on oven tray, decorate with pastry trimmings. Brush top and sides with egg white. Bake in moderate oven 45 to 50 minutes; cool.

AVOCADO AND DILL SALAD

1 butter lettuce
1 avocado
1 carrot, grated
1 cup alfalfa sprouts
2 dill pickles
DRESSING
¼ cup olive oil
1 egg yolk

1 teaspoon vinegar
1 tablespoon lemon juice
1 teaspoon French mustard
½ teaspoon sugar
2 tablespoons chopped fresh dill
1 small clove garlic, crushed

Wash lettuce, line 2 individual bowls with outer leaves, tear remaining leaves into pieces, toss with carrot, sprouts and dill pickles, cut into long thin strips, and half the chopped avocado. Slice remaining half of avocado. Place salad into bowls, top with sliced avocado, brush with some of the Dressing, cover with plastic food wrap. Pour remaining Dressing over salad just before serving.

Dressing: Combine all ingredients in blender or food processor, blend until smooth. Place in screw-top jar, shake well before using.

Family Picnic

Appetites are particularly healthy in the open air, so make sure you have enough food to suit your family's requirements. We suggest a soup for the cooler months; serve it as soon as you reach your destination. Quantities are for six people.

PUMPKIN AND CUMIN SOUP
1 oz butter
2 onions, chopped
2 teaspoons ground cumin
2 chicken stock cubes
3 cups water
1 butternut pumpkin (about 2 lb)
pinch nutmeg
1 tablespoon chopped chives

Heat butter in pan, add onion, cook until transparent, add cumin, cook, stirring for 2 minutes. Add crumbled stock cubes, water, peeled and chopped pumpkin and nutmeg. Cover, simmer 15 minutes or until pumpkin is tender. Puree soup in blender or processor. Reheat, pour into vacuum flask to keep hot for picnic. Serve sprinkled with chives.

AURORA COLESLAW

Combine vegetables and pineapple the day before required, add cheese and dressing up to two hours before serving.

4 cups finely shredded cabbage
1 medium onion, finely chopped
2 x 8¼-oz cans pineapple
    chunks, drained
1 small red bell pepper, finely
    chopped
1 small green bell pepper,
    finely chopped
1 cup grated cheddar cheese
½ cup mayonnaise
2 tablespoons lemon juice
½ cup cream, whipped

Combine cabbage, onion, pineapple, peppers and cheese in container. Refrigerate, covered, 2 hours.

Combine mayonnaise with lemon juice, fold in cream. Pour over cabbage and toss well.

SEASONED CHICKEN DRUMSTICKS

12 chicken drumsticks
3 bacon slices, chopped
3 zucchini, grated
½ x 6-oz package Seasoned
    Stuffing Mix
1 egg
2 oz butter

Place bacon in heated pan, cook, stirring until crisp. Add zucchini, cook 2 minutes stirring, add Stuffing Mix, mix well. Remove from heat, cool 5 minutes. Stir in lightly beaten egg.

Loosen skin around each chicken leg with fingers. Push about a tablespoon of stuffing mixture firmly under skin. Melt butter in baking dish, add chicken legs, brushing tops with some of the butter. Bake in moderately hot oven 15 minutes, reduce to moderate, bake further 40 minutes or until golden brown and tender. Baste frequently with pan juices during cooking.

TOMATO SALAD WITH CREAMY TARRAGON DRESSING

If preferred, use 2 teaspoons of chopped mint instead of basil.

1 lb tomatoes, thinly sliced
2 shallots, chopped
CREAMY TARRAGON DRESSING
⅔ cup oil
⅓ cup tarragon white wine
    vinegar
2 tablespoons sour cream
1 teaspoon French mustard
1 clove garlic, crushed
1 tablespoon chopped parsley
1 tablespoon chopped basil

Arrange tomatoes on serving plate or in container, pour Dressing over, sprinkle with shallots.

Creamy Tarragon Dressing: Combine all ingredients in jar, shake well.

PIZZA LOAF

Use a soft strasbourg salami to ensure easy slicing of loaf.

DOUGH
2 cups all-purpose flour
¼ oz sachet dried yeast
1 teaspoon sugar
¾ cup warm water
FILLING
4 slices mozzarella cheese
15 slices soft salami
½ cup tomato sauce
½ teaspoon dried oregano leaves
½ lb broccoli
1 egg
10-oz jar sliced red peppers
4 oz pepperoni salami, in 1 piece
20 stuffed olives

Dough: Make well in sifted flour, stir in combined yeast, sugar and water, mix to a firm dough, knead for about 5 minutes on floured surface until smooth and elastic. Using ¾ of the dough, roll out to a rectangle large enough to line a greased 3½x8½-inch loaf pan, leave ¾ inch of dough over edge.

Filling: Place a layer of mozzarella evenly over dough, top with rolled-up soft salami. Pour over combined tomato sauce and oregano. Break broccoli into small flowerets, drop into pan of boiling water, boil 1 minute, refresh under cold water. Arrange broccoli over tomato sauce, top evenly with beaten egg. Drain peppers well, place over broccoli. Remove skin from pepperoni, slice very thinly, arrange neatly over red peppers. Cut olives in half lengthways, place in a row down center of the loaf.

Roll out remaining pizza dough large enough to cover top of loaf, place on top, join edges with a little water, pinch together. Decorate top with scraps of dough, cut a few slits to allow steam to escape. Bake in moderately hot oven 40 minutes. Remove from pan, place onto an oven tray, bake further 10 minutes to brown sides. Cover top with aluminum foil if it is getting too brown. Allow to become cold before cutting.

GOLDEN CARROT FRUIT CAKE

Make and frost this cake a day before it is needed. Store in airtight container. Cake will freeze well for up to a month.

2 oz butter
2 teaspoons grated orange rind
⅓ cup brown sugar
2 eggs
⅓ cup golden syrup
1 cup coarsely grated carrot
2 slices glacé pineapple, finely chopped
2 whole glacé apricots, finely chopped
¼ cup seedless raisins
¼ cup coconut
⅔ cup all-purpose flour
⅔ cup self-rising flour
½ teaspoon mixed spice
⅓ cup orange juice
ORANGE CHEESE FROSTING
2 oz packaged cream cheese
1 oz butter
2 teaspoons orange juice
2 cups powdered sugar

Cream butter, orange rind and sugar until light and creamy, then add eggs one at a time, beating well after each addition; beat in golden syrup. Stir in carrot, fruit and coconut, then sifted flours and spice alternately with orange juice. Spread into greased 8-inch ring pan that has base lined with greaseproof paper. Bake in moderate oven 50 to 60 minutes, cool in tin. When cold, frost with Orange Cheese Frosting.

Orange Cheese Frosting: Beat cheese, butter and orange juice together until smooth and creamy, gradually beat in sifted powdered sugar, beat until smooth.

Many people these days prefer to cater for their own Wedding Breakfast at home. Our menu is for 50 guests; follow the pointers at the beginning of each recipe. You will know your own guests best, but we have given the recipes in manageable quantities that you can halve or double. It is usually best to make only the given quantities at any one time. Serve sherry with the three savories we've suggested. Each recipe makes about 24 savories. Double each recipe to allow about three savories per person.

Double each quantity of salad; combined they will be adequate for 50.

The Shrimp and Avocado Salad in the given quantity will serve 50, along with the other two main courses.

The Cherry Duck Roll is wonderful to look at and tastes great—make two.

Each of the suggested desserts will serve ten. It's difficult to estimate how much dessert people will eat—they usually want to try both—so either make three of each and cut them into smaller servings, or make five of each and leave the servings generous.

A cheese and fruit platter, served with coffee to finish the meal, will please your guests, and of course, the grand finale will be the Croquembouche.

CHERRY DUCK ROLL

This is the best way we know to make a duck (or a chicken) stretch a long way. You should get about 40 slices from one duck, depending on how thickly it is sliced. Boning the duck is easy once you begin. Use a sharp pointed knife and go slowly to prevent cutting the skin. The Rolls can be made and kept covered and refrigerated up to two days before required. We recommend you do two of the Rolls. Serve on a bed of lettuce.

3¼-lb duck
4 shallots, chopped
1 clove garlic, crushed
2 oz butter
1 cup stale bread crumbs
5 chicken breast fillets, ground
3 bacon slices, ground
¼ cup chopped parsley
1 egg
½ x 14-oz can pitted black cherries, drained
1 tablespoon oil
1 tablespoon gelatin
1 cup water
½ teaspoon soy sauce

Sauté shallots and garlic in butter for 1 minute. In a bowl, combine shallot mixture, bread crumbs, chicken, bacon, parsley and egg.

STEP 1
Using a small sharp knife, cut off wing tips at second joint. Then cut through skin of duck down center back. Separate flesh from backbone on one side with tip of knife. Then, following shape of bones of duck, gradually ease flesh away from bones. Repeat process with other side of duck.

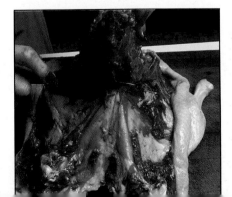

STEP 2
Holding the rib cage away from duck, gently cut breastbone from flesh

STEP 3
Hold up the thigh with one hand, cut around top of bone to remove flesh, scrape down the bone to the next joint, cut around flesh again, scrape down to the end. Pull bone out and cut away. Repeat this process with other leg bone and with both wings. Turn flesh of legs and wings inside duck.

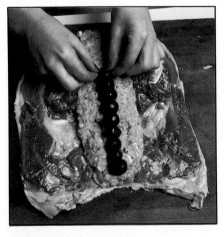

STEP 4
Spoon half the bread crumb mixture down center of duck, place cherries down center as shown, then cover with remaining half of mixture.

STEP 5
Fold one side of duck over bread crumb mixture, then other side.

STEP 6
Sew the flesh, using a needle and dark thread. Tie with string at 2-inch intervals to keep shape while cooking. Place duck in a baking dish, rub with oil. Bake uncovered in moderate oven 1¼ hours, stand 20 minutes, then remove string and thread, cool, refrigerate covered overnight. Garnish duck with shallots. Add gelatin to water, dissolve over hot water, add soy sauce. Stand until glaze begins to thicken. Brush over duck, refrigerate until set.

SEASONED BACON ROLLS

Prepare rolls the day before required, keep refrigerated, covered.

12 bacon slices
2½ cups stale bread crumbs
1 Granny Smith apple, grated
¼ cup chopped chives
¾ cup grated cheddar cheese
1 egg
pepper

Cut bacon slices in half. Combine bread crumbs with apple, chives, cheese, lightly beaten egg and pepper, mix well. Roll tablespoonfuls of mixture into sausage shapes about 1½ inches long, wrap in a piece of bacon, secure end with toothpick. Place on wire rack over baking dish, bake in moderately hot oven 20 to 30 minutes or until golden brown.

Makes 24 rolls.

HOT POLISH SAUSAGE KEBABS

Soak skewers overnight in cold water. Assemble kebabs and prepare soy sauce, basting mixture the day before required, cover, refrigerate.

12 oz cooked Polish sausages
2 green bell peppers
2 x 8¼-oz cans sliced pineapple
2 teaspoons soy sauce
1 teaspoon lemon juice
2 teaspoons honey
1 tablespoon ginger wine

Cut sausages, peppers and drained pineapple into ¼-inch pieces. Place onto bamboo skewers. Bake in moderate oven 10 minutes brushing often with combined soy sauce, lemon juice, honey and ginger wine.

Makes about 24 kebabs.

SMOKED SALMON AND CAMEMBERT ROUNDS

Bake bread rounds up to a week before the wedding. When cold, store in airtight container. Complete savories up to several hours before required, cover, refrigerate. Bake just before ready to serve.

12 slices white bread
10 oz butter melted
4 oz butter, extra
2 teaspoons lemon juice
2 tablespoons chopped fresh dill
4 oz smoked salmon
2 x 4-oz wheels Camembert cheese
red or black caviar

Cut 2 2-inch circles from each slice of bread. Brush both sides of circles lightly with melted butter, place on oven tray. Bake in moderate oven 10 minutes or until golden brown; cool.

Beat extra butter until creamy, beat in lemon juice and dill, spread on bread rounds, top with small piece of smoked salmon, then a wedge of Camembert cheese.

Bake in moderate oven 5 to 7 minutes or until cheese is just beginning to melt. Garnish with dill or caviar.

Makes 24.

POTATO SALAD WITH SALMON DRESSING
4¼ small white potatoes
6 shallots, sliced
12 hard-boiled eggs, quartered
½ x 1-lb jar gherkins, sliced
SALMON DRESSING
2 x 7½-oz cans red salmon, drained
1-lb jar tartar sauce
2 tablespoons chopped mint

Boil or steam potatoes until tender, remove skins, place in salad bowl, add shallots, eggs, gherkins, pour Dressing over, toss lightly and serve.

Salmon Dressing: Puree salmon and tartar sauce in processor or blender, add mint, process until smooth.

Serves 12.

BROWN AND WHITE RICE SALAD
1½ cups brown rice
1½ cups white rice
2 x 8¼-oz cans pineapple pieces
2 red bell peppers, sliced
1 green bell pepper, chopped
14½-oz can corn kernels, drained
2 stalks celery, sliced
½ cup French dressing

Add brown rice gradually to large pan of boiling water, boil rapidly uncovered for 30 minutes or until as tender as desired; drain, rinse under cold water, drain. Add white rice gradually to large pan of boiling water, boil rapidly uncovered for 10 minutes or until tender; drain, rinse under cold water, drain. Drain pineapple, reserve ¼ cup syrup. Combine rice with peppers, corn, celery and pineapple. Combine reserved pineapple syrup with French dressing. Pour over rice mixture just before serving.

Serves 12.

SPINACH AND PECAN SALAD
12 spinach leaves, shredded
½ lb cherry tomatoes
1 onion, sliced
10-oz can cannellini beans, drained
7 oz pecans
DRESSING
2 egg yolks
2 teaspoons lemon juice
2 tablespoons white vinegar
2 teaspoons honey
½ cup oil
½ teaspoon dried basil leaves
¼ teaspoon dried tarragon leaves

Combine spinach with tomatoes, onion and rinsed beans. Add Dressing, sprinkle with pecans just before serving.

Dressing: Whisk egg yolks with lemon juice, vinegar and honey, place in screw-top jar, add remaining ingredients, shake well.

Serves 12.

APRICOT-GLAZED LEG HAM

We ordered a 17-lb leg of ham for the wedding. Cut the skin with a sharp knife in a pattern, as shown at right, then neatly and carefully remove the rest of the skin by slipping your hand underneath and releasing it from the fat. Keep the skin to cover any leftover ham to prevent it from drying out. Brush the fat with combined ½ cup strained apricot jam and 1 tablespoon brandy. Bake in moderately hot oven 20 to 30 minutes or until jam looks slightly set. We decorated our ham with red pepper flowers, shallot strips, whole cloves and sliced radishes. We put the decorations on after baking. However, if the decorations had been large, such as orange and pineapple slices, cherries, etc., the ham could be decorated before baking. Make sure the ham can be carved easily by supporting it on a spiked meat dish or ham stand.

SHRIMP AND AVOCADO SALAD WITH DILL DRESSING

Prepare shrimp and Dressing the day before required. Leave slicing of avocado until just ready to serve, then top with Dressing to prevent discoloration.

7½ lb cooked jumbo shrimp
8 ripe avocados, peeled, sliced
4 lettuce leaves
DILL DRESSING
½ pint sour cream
1 cup mayonnaise
1 cup French dressing
2 tablespoons chopped chives
2 tablespoons chopped fresh dill

Peel and devein shrimp, arrange on lettuce-covered serving plate with avocado, pour Dressing over top.
Dill Dressing: Whisk all ingredients together.

CHOCOLATE STRAWBERRY MOUSSE CAKE

Complete cake up to 48 hours before serving, keep refrigerated, covered and left in the pan. Each cake will cut into 10 slices.

Chocolate Sponge Cake (see page 82)
½ pint whipping cream
2 oz semisweet baking chocolate
½ lb strawberries
STRAWBERRY MOUSSE
½ lb strawberries
½ cup fine granulated sugar
1 envelope unflavored gelatin
2 tablespoons lemon juice
2 egg whites
½ cup whipping cream
1 tablespoon Grand Marnier

Make sponge according to recipe on page 82. Pour mixture into greased 15x10-inch Swiss roll pan, bake in moderate oven 15 to 20 minutes, turn onto rack to cool. Line a 8x4x3-inch loaf pan with aluminum foil, cut pieces of cake to line base and long sides of pan. Cake should extend 1 inch above top edge of pan. Pour in Mousse, push three-quarters of the strawberries into Mousse. Place a layer of cake on top of Mousse. Refrigerate, covered, overnight. To serve, turn cake onto serving plate. Combine cream and chocolate, heat chocolate without boiling until chocolate is melted. Refrigerate 30 minutes, then beat on electric mixer until soft peaks form. Do not overbeat or cream will curdle. Cover cake with cream, decorate with remaining cream and strawberries.
Strawberry Mousse: Puree, blend or process strawberries and sugar until smooth. Dissolve gelatin in lemon juice over hot water, pour into strawberry mixture. Fold in beaten egg whites, then whipped cream and Grand Marnier.

LEMON MERINGUE CREAM

Make meringue shells up to a two weeks before required. Store when cold in an airtight container. Fill, decorate and refrigerate up to 12 hours before serving. Filling can be made a few days before required. Store, covered—not in an aluminum pan—in refrigerator. Decorate each meringue case with fresh fruit and whipped cream. You will need about 1 cup cream, whipped until firm peaks form, then piped decoratively into shell. Each meringue case will cut into 10 wedges. Make between 3 and 5 meringue cases.

4 egg whites
1¼ cups sugar
1 teaspoon lemon juice
2 teaspoons powdered sugar
FILLING
5 tablespoons cornstarch
½ cup sugar
1 cup water
2 teaspoons grated lemon rind
⅓ cup lemon juice
10 oz butter
4 egg yolks
½ cup cream

Cut 9½ inch circle from piece of greaseproof paper; place on lightly greased oven tray. Brush paper lightly with melted butter, dust with cornstarch, shake off excess.

Combine egg whites, sugar and lemon juice in small bowl of electric mixer, beat on high speed for 15 minutes. Fold in sifted powdered sugar. Spread a ¼-inch layer of meringue over prepared paper. Pipe remaining meringue mixture around edge to form shell. Bake in very slow oven 1 to 1½ hours or until dry to touch; cool in oven with door ajar. Remove paper from meringue, place on serving plate. Spread Filling into meringue shell, refrigerate until set. Decorate with whipped cream and fruit.

Filling: Blend cornstarch and sugar with water, lemon rind and lemon juice in pan. Stir constantly over heat until mixture boils and thickens, reduce heat, simmer, stirring, 1 minute. Remove from heat, stir in butter, then egg yolks, cover, cool to room temperature. Stir in cream. Press a piece of plastic food wrap onto surface of Filling to prevent skin from forming.

CROQUEMBOUCHE

To make a spectacular Croquembouche (French wedding cake) is not as difficult as it may seem, and it is becoming a popular breakaway from the traditional fruitcake. It will be necessary to buy a Croquembouche cone on which to assemble the puffs. The one we used is stainless steel and costs about $40 at shops that stock commercial kitchenware. The cone stands 14 inches high, and its base measures 9 inches.

The completed Croquembouche will stand up well in a cool place; do not refrigerate, as toffee will soften. If the weather is hot or humid, the Croquembouche must be assembled even closer to serving time than the 6 hours suggested.

The important thing to remember when making puffs is that if they are cooked properly, doughy centers will result in softened puffs. They can be made up to a month before required and frozen in airtight bags, or stored in an airtight container for up to a week. If they soften, recrisp uncovered on trays in a moderate oven for a few minutes. Fill them with cream as close to assembling time as possible, no longer than 1 hour.

Sort out the puffs into large, medium and small groups and start at the base of the cone with the largest puffs. The Croquembouche is quite quick and easy to assemble, particularly with another pair of helping hands.

Any leftover puffs can be served first, before breaking into the Croquembouche. Use two forks to gently pull away the puffs from the cone; serve two puffs per person with some extra whipped cream.

CHOUX PUFFS
3 cups water
7 oz butter
3 cups all-purpose flour
12 eggs
FILLING
2 x ½-pint cartons cream
½ cup powdered sugar
2 tablespoons Grand Marnier
2 teaspoons grated orange rind
CARAMEL
2 cups water
4 cups sugar

STEP 1
Cut butter into pieces of about the same size. Combine 1 cup of the water and 2½ oz of the butter in pan, bring to boil, stirring until butter melts. Add 1 cup of the flour all at once, stir vigorously with wooden spoon until mixture leaves side of pan and forms a smooth ball; remove from heat. Cool slightly, add 4 of the beaten eggs, a little at a time, beating well after each addition. This can be done on an electric mixer of food processor. Mixture should be smooth and glossy. Drip slightly rounded teaspoons of mixture, about 2 inches apart, onto lightly greased oven trays. Bake in hot oven 10 minutes, reduce heat to moderate, bake further 15 to 20 minutes, or until golden brown and crisp. Remove from oven, make small slits in sides of Puffs to allow steam to escape; return to moderate oven for a few minutes to dry out. Repeat process twice with remaining Choux Puff ingredients. When preparing last quantity of Puffs, spoon ½ teaspoonfuls of mixture onto trays to give small Puffs. These are used to fill in small gaps when layering the Puffs.

STEP 2
Filling: Whip cream and powdered sugar until stiff peaks form; fold in Grand Marnier and orange rind. Make a small hole in bottom of each Puff with finger. Place cream into piping bag fitted with a small plain tube, pipe a little cream into each Puff.

STEP 3
Caramel: Place half the sugar and half the water in frying pan, stir over heat without boiling until sugar is dissolved. Bring to boil, boil rapidly without stirring until mixture turns golden brown. Place Croquembouche cone on plate, dip bottom of each puff into Caramel; arrange around cone in layers, using the largest Puffs first.

STEP 4
Decorate Croquembouche with crystallized violets (to prepare violets see page 69 or buy them from a gourmet delicatessen) by dipping backs of violets in Caramel. Make another quantity of Caramel using the remaining ingredients. Drizzle Croquembouche with cooled Caramel. Let stand at room temperature, no longer than 6 hours.

The menu for this party would be perfect for an at-home young person's celebration, such as a birthday or an engagement party. Our party is planned for 25 guests. Have a look at the Punches section for some interesting suggestions on what to serve for drinks. We've suggested two dips for starters; serve these with savory crackers, chips and crisp fresh vegetables. If you decide to serve other nibbles, such as olives, salami, etc., then one quantity of each dip will be enough, but if the dips are served alone, double the quantity for each recipe. For an entrée, serve the vegetarian-style lasagna—it's hearty and tasty. Cut each quantity into eight to ten servings.

Serve a choice of two main courses for your guests. The quantities given for each recipe will serve twelve generously. Both recipes can be doubled, but you'll find them easier to handle if you make them in two batches. You will know your guests' appetites best.

Make three of the apple flans—they're always popular—and a large bowl of fruit salad spiked with champagne. Serve coffee and the cake to end a delicious meal.

TARAMA OLIVE DIP

This dip can be prepared up to 12 hours ahead. Leave out olives until ready to serve. Serve with crackers or crunchy pieces of fresh vegetables.

8-oz package cream cheese
8-oz container taramansalata (or combination of roe, garlic and olive oil)
2 teaspoons lemon juice
2 tablespoons finely chopped black olives

Beat cream cheese until smooth in electric mixer of food processor. Beat in taramansalata and lemon juice. Stir in black olives just before serving.

AVOCADO CREAM DIP

Prepare up to 12 hours before serving, cover, refrigerate

2 ripe avocados, mashed
2 cloves garlic, crushed
1 tablespoon lime or lemon juice
½ cup sour cream
2 tablespoons mayonnaise
1 small red bell pepper, chopped
2 shallots, chopped
1 teaspoon horseradish cream
dash Tabasco sauce

Combine avocado, garlic, lime juice, sour cream and mayonnaise in processor or mixer, beat until smooth. Stir in red pepper, shallots, horseradish cream and the dash of Tabasco.

CHEESY VEGETABLE LASAGNA

Prepare a day ahead, cover, refrigerate, bake 45 minutes before ready to serve, stand 10 minutes before cutting. Make 3 quantities to serve 25 guests. This recipe is not suitable for freezing.

TOMATO SAUCE
1 tablespoon oil
1 onion, chopped
8 oz mushrooms, sliced
1 small green bell pepper, chopped
1 teaspoon dried basil leaves
½ teaspoon dried oregano leaves
14½-oz can tomatoes
½ cup tomato paste
2 tomatoes, peeled, chopped
½ teaspoon sugar
½ x 6½-oz package cooked lasagna noodles
WHITE WINE SAUCE
10 oz butter
2 tablespoons all-purpose flour
2 tablespoons dry white wine
¾ cup milk
½ cup grated cheddar cheese
SPINACH LAYER
12 spinach leaves, chopped
1 tablespoon oil
1 clove garlic, crushed
2 shallots, chopped
CHEESE LAYER
13 oz ricotta cheese
½ cup grated Parmesan cheese
2 eggs

Tomato Sauce: Heat oil, add onion, mushrooms and green pepper, cook and stir over high heat until onion is tender, about 3 minutes. Add herbs, undrained crushed tomatoes, tomato paste, tomatoes and sugar, bring to boil, reduce heat, simmer uncovered 30 minutes, stirring occasionally. Pour half the Tomato Sauce into a 6½ x 10-inch pan or ovenproof dish. Place a single layer of noodles over Tomato Sauce, then Spinach Layer, then Cheese Layer. Top with a second layer of noodles, then remaining Tomato Sauce. Pour White Wine Sauce over Tomato Sauce. Bake, uncovered, for 30 minutes in moderately hot oven or until top is bubbly and beginning to brown. Stand 10 minutes before cutting.

White Wine Sauce: Melt butter in pan, stir in flour, cook 1 minute stirring. Gradually stir in wine and milk, stir over heat until Sauce boils and thickens, add cheese, stir until melted.

Spinach Layer: Heat oil in pan, add garlic, spinach and shallots. Stir-fry until spinach is wilted, about 3 minutes; drain away as much liquid as possible.

Cheese Layer: Beat cheese and eggs together until blended.

CREAMY CHICKEN AND MUSHROOMS

This recipe is so easy it's not worthwhile preparing it ahead. It looks at its best made up to about 3 hours beforehand and reheated when ready to serve. The chicken and vegetables can be chopped and sliced the day before required.

3 barbecued chickens
10 oz butter
1 lb mushrooms, sliced
6 shallots, sliced
¼ cup port
2½ x 10¾-oz cans cream of
    mushroom soup
1½ cups milk
1 teaspoon Worcestershire sauce
¼ teaspoon cayenne pepper
2 x ½-pint cartons sour cream

Cut chicken meat into 1-inch pieces. Heat butter in pan, add mushrooms and shallots, cook until mushrooms are just soft, about 5 minutes. Add port, undiluted soup, milk, Worcestershire sauce and cayenne pepper. Bring to boil, add chicken and sour cream, reduce to low, cook until chicken is heated through.

TOMATO LAMB CURRY

We have given 1 tablespoon curry powder so it is a subtle flavor; increase to suit your guests' tastes. Prepare curry up to two days before serving, or it can be frozen. Leave onion-garlic curry mixture out until thawing curry, then fry off mixture and incorporate it into lamb mixture. Leave parsley and almonds out until ready to serve, whether freezing or refrigerating. We accompanied the curry with a good mango chutney, combined sliced green and red pepper and onion rings, sliced bananas, dipped in lime juice then in toasted coconut, and Yogurt Cucumber. Serve with Saffron Rice.

2 boned legs of lamb
   (about 2¼ lb each)
2 tablespoons oil
4 cloves garlic, crushed
10 medium onions, quartered
1 tablespoon curry powder
3 x 14½-oz cans tomatoes
3 teaspoons cornstarch
2 tablespoons water
3 oz blanched almonds
1 oz butter
3 tablespoons chopped parsley

Trim away excess fat from lamb, cut into 1-inch cubes. Heat oil in large pan, gradually add enough lamb to cover base of pan in single layer, cook over high heat stirring until golden brown all over,

remove from pan. Repeat with remaining lamb until all is well browned. It is important to fry meat well. Add garlic, onions and curry powder to pan, stir constantly until onion is lightly browned. Add undrained, crushed tomatoes. Stir until mixture boils, combine all these ingredients in large pan, cover, simmer 1 hour or until lamb is tender. Stir several times during cooking.

Stir in blended cornstarch and water, stir until mixture boils and thickens. Place almonds and butter in another pan, stir over heat until almonds are lightly browned, drain on kitchen paper. Serve lamb sprinkled with almonds and parsley

YOGURT CUCUMBER
2 cucumbers, peeled, sliced
1 teaspoon salt
½ cup plain natural yogurt
Combine cucumbers with salt, stand 30 minutes; rinse cucumbers under cold water; drain well, combine with yogurt.

SAFFRON RICE
3 cups long-grain rice
1 oz butter
tiny pinch saffron powder
2 tablespoons chopped parsley
Cook rice in boiling salted water 12 minutes or until tender, drain. Add butter, saffron and parsley while rice is still hot.

APPLE AND PASSION FRUIT FLAN

Apple pies are always a hit. This is just an updated version. One pie will cut into eight wedges; make three for your guests up to a day before serving, or make pastry and refrigerate, in or out of the pie pans, for up to a week.

WALNUT PASTRY
4 oz butter
1⅓ cups all-purpose flour
¾ cup ground walnuts
⅓ cup sugar
2 egg yolks
FILLING
2 x 15-oz cans pie apple
2 passion fruit
1 teaspoon cinnamon
3 small Granny Smith apples, peeled
½ cup apricot jam
Walnut Pastry: Rub butter into sifted flour, mix in walnuts and sugar, then egg yolks, mix quickly into a firm dough, knead lightly on floured surface until smooth, cover, refrigerate 30 minutes. Line 9-inch flan tin with pastry. Spread pie-apple mixture into flan case, top with sliced apple. Bake in moderate oven 45 minutes. Brush with jam.

Filling: Combine apple, pulp of passion fruit and cinnamon in food processor, process until smooth. Slice quartered apples thinly. Heat and strain jam.

CELEBRATION CAKE

We chose the easy way to decorate a cake. Make your own favorite rich fruit-cake. We used a recipe based on ½ pound of butter and cooked it in a 9-inch round cake pan. Make the cake at least a week before the party. Place the cake on a board covered with pretty paper, brush the cake thoroughly with lightly beaten egg white. Roll out about 24-ounce package almond paste on a surface that has been dusted with pure powdered sugar. Leave the cake for a day, brush lightly but evenly with egg white and cover with 24 ounces of packaged soft icing. This is available—like the almond paste—at health food stores and most supermarkets. We colored our icing with some yellow food coloring; it is simply kneaded into the soft icing with some sifted pure powdered sugar. The soft icing rolls out easily, just like pastry. Trim the edges and leave the cake for another day. To decorate the cake, choose a ribbon of contrasting color, buy some extra for the handle of the knife and attach it to the cake with pins. Make a bow and cover the joint by pinning the bow to the cake. Decorate with artificial or real flowers—or explain to a florist what you want and he or she will make a suitable bouquet. The cake is finished with a piped edge and writing. These are not necessary but nicely add the finishing touch. A basic plastic piping kit is available from department stores if you want to attempt a little cake decorating.

CHAMPAGNE FRUIT SALAD

Use any combination of seasonal fruits of your choice. Combine fruit and sugar syrup up to 12 hours before serving, keep refrigerated. Add chilled champagne just before serving. There is good-quality fruit salad available in large quantities. If time is short, buy about 4½ pounds of fruit salad and add some passion fruit or whatever fruit it needs to look more glamorous.

- 4 oranges
- 4 apples
- 4 bananas
- 4 passion fruit
- 4 kiwifruit
- 2 cantaloupes
- 1 lb grapes
- 1½ lb strawberries
- 1 pineapple
- ½ cup lemon juice
- 3 cups water
- 1 cup sugar
- 750ml bottle dry champagne

Peel and chop fruit into chunky pieces of uniform size. Combine lemon juice, water and sugar in pan, stir over heat until sugar is dissolved, bring to boil, remove from heat. Cool to room temperature, pour over fruit salad. Top with chilled champagne just before serving.

GARDEN PARTY

Choose a warm evening to have a garden party. Serve a variety of drinks from cocktails to champagne with bite-sized savories. Each of our savory recipes will make about 20. Choose which ones you like and allow for each person to eat about 6 savories and about 2 of the sweet treats. Serve these with coffee at party's end.

STUFFED CHERRY TOMATOES

Prepare up to 2 hours before serving

20 cherry tomatoes
3 oz black olives, finely chopped
1 clove garlic, crushed
3 teaspoons French dressing
3 shallots, finely chopped

Cut a thick slice from top of each tomato. Using a teaspoon, scoop out and discard half the pulp. Combine olives, garlic, French dressing and shallots. Fill tomatoes with olive mixture.

Serve at room temperature.

SMOKED SALMON AND CUCUMBER CANAPÉS

Prepare cucumber and salmon mixture the day before required, refrigerate, covered. Pipe mixture onto cucumber up to 2 hours before serving; keep canapés covered and refrigerated.

2 thin cucumbers
3 slices smoked salmon
2 oz packaged cream cheese
1 tablespoon chopped fresh dill

Peel cucumbers, remove seeds with apple corer or knife. Cut into slices about ¼ inch thick; you need about 20 slices. Process smoked salmon with cream cheese and dill. Using a fluted pipe and bag, pipe salmon mixture around top of each slice of cucumber.

Makes about 20.

TURKEY AND PÂTÉ ROLLS

We used bottled or canned red peppers to garnish these rolls. The pâté can be made up to four days before required.

½ lb pumpernickel bread rounds
1 oz butter
6 oz sliced turkey breast roll
1 cup chopped parsley
bottled red peppers
PÂTÉ
12 oz chicken livers
2 tablespoons port
1 onion, chopped
10 oz butter
½ teaspoon mixed herbs
3 oz butter, extra
¼ cup cream
salt, pepper

AVOCADO AND SMOKED SALMON ROLLS

Prepare, cover, refrigerate up to 3 hours before serving.

1 small avocado
4 oz ricotta cheese
¼ cup sour cream
1 teaspoon lemon juice
salt, pepper
6½ oz sliced smoked salmon
¼ cup chopped fresh dill

Combine avocado pulp, ricotta cheese, sour cream, lemon juice, salt and pepper in processor, process until smooth.

Spread avocado mixture onto slices of smoked salmon. Roll up like a Swiss roll, cut into 1-inch lengths. Secure each roll with a toothpick. Spread ends of each roll with avocado mixture, dip into the chopped dill.

Makes about 20.

OYSTER-STUFFED MUSHROOMS

Choose mushrooms just large enough to hold an oyster. Sauce can be made, covered and refrigerated up to a day before required.

20 oysters
20 mushrooms
SAUCE
2 ripe tomatoes, chopped
2 shallots, chopped
1 tablespoon red wine vinegar

Remove stems from mushrooms; place 1 oyster into cavity of each mushroom. Spoon Sauce over oysters.
Sauce: Combine tomatoes, shallots and vinegar in pan, stir until mixture boils, reduce heat, simmer covered 10 minutes. Blend or process until smooth, strain, reheat to serve over oysters.

Makes 20.

Place a small dab of butter in center of pumpernickel rounds. Spread a thin layer of pâté over 3 slices of turkey, sandwich together. Spread pâté over top of turkey slices, press parsley over top, roll up like a Swiss roll, trim ends. Repeat with remaining turkey slices and pâté. Cut into ¼-inch-thick slices, place 1 slice on each round of bread. Garnish with strips of red pepper.
Pate: Marinate cleaned livers in wine for 1 hour. Sauté onion in butter until tender, add herbs and undrained livers, cook 5 minutes. Add extra butter, stir until melted. Add cream, season with salt and pepper. Puree, process or blend pâté until smooth, pour into bowl, cover, refrigerate until firm.

Makes about 20.

MINI CHEESE AND BACON BISCUITS

Biscuits are at their best made, baked and served, but they're almost as good made up to 12 hours before serving. Make them, place in tin, top with cheese and olives, cover and refrigerate. Cook straight from refrigerator as directed below.

2 bacon slices, finely chopped
1 oz butter
1½ cups self-rising flour
1 teaspoon sugar
1 tablespoon chopped chives
½ cup milk, approximately
1 oz butter, extra
grated Parmesan cheese
stuffed olives

Saute bacon in pan until crisp, cool. Rub butter into sifted flour and sugar. Add bacon, chives and enough milk to mix to a soft, sticky dough. Turn onto lightly floured surface, knead lightly until smooth, press out to ½ inch in depth. Cut into rounds with 1-inch cutter. Place biscuits into 7x10-inch pan. Brush tops with extra melted butter, sprinkle with cheese, top with a slice of stuffed olive. Bake in very hot oven 10 to 15 minutes. Serve hot with butter.

Makes about 24.

SPICY PINEAPPLE MEATBALLS

Cook meatballs the day before required. Reheat, covered, in moderate oven for about 20 minutes.

12 oz ground steak
dash Tabasco
1 teaspoon Worcestershire sauce
1 clove garlic, crushed
½ small Granny Smith
apple, peeled, grated
¼ cup stale bread crumbs
oil for shallow frying
2 x 8 ¼-oz cans pineapple chunks

Combine ground steak with Tabasco, Worcestershire sauce, garlic, apple and bread crumbs, mix well. Shape mixture into balls, roll in flour; shallow fry in hot oil until golden brown all over. Top each meatball with a piece of pineapple.

Makes about 20 balls.

SMOKED HAM CORNETS

Prepare several hours before required, keep covered in refrigerator. Garnish with caviar just before serving.

1 lb packaged cream cheese
2 teaspoons French Mustard
1 tablespoon brandy
2 tablespoons chopped chives
⅓ cup finely chopped walnuts
20 slices smoked ham

Beat cream cheese, mustard and brandy until smooth, stir in chives and walnuts. Roll ham into cone shapes. Using piping bag and plain tube, pipe cream cheese mixture into ham cones.

Garnish with caviar, if desired.
Makes 20.

SHRIMP TOASTS WITH DILL BUTTER

We used small shrimp for this recipe.

5 slices white bread
4 oz butter
1 teaspoon lemon juice
½ teaspoon dried basil leaves
1 tablespoon chopped parsley
1 tablespoon chopped fresh dill
1 lb cooked shrimp, shelled

Toast bread, remove crusts, spread toast generously with combined butter, lemon juice, basil, parsley and dill. Cut each piece of toast into 4 squares. Top with halved prawns. Garnish with tiny lemon or lime wedges, caviar and dill.

Makes 20.

CHICKEN AND ASPARAGUS ROLLS

1 large chicken breast fillet
3 teaspoons mayonnaise
salt, pepper
2 tablespoons stale bread crumbs
1 sheet ready rolled puff pastry
10½-oz can asparagus spears, drained
1 egg
2 tablespoons sesame seeds

Process chopped chicken with mayonnaise, salt, pepper and bread crumbs until smooth. Place mixture into piping bag fitted with plain ⅜-inch tube. Roll pastry 1 way only, to give a rectangle 10x14-inch. Cut pastry lengthwise into 3 even strips. Pipe chicken mixture along edge of each strip of pastry. Place asparagus spears in single row alongside chicken. Brush pastry with beaten egg. Roll pastry over filling to enclose filling completely. Brush top with egg, cut rolls diagonally into 1¼ pieces, sprinkle with sesame seeds, place on greased oven trays. Bake in hot oven 10 minutes, reduce heat to moderate, bake further 10 minutes or until golden brown.

Makes about 20.

SEASONED BUTTON MUSHROOMS

Prepare Seasoning up to a day before required; fill mushrooms up to several hours before serving.

20 small mushrooms
mayonnaise
SEASONING
1 bacon slice, finely chopped
½ stick celery, finely chopped
2 shallots, finely sliced
1 small clove garlic, crushed
1 tablespoon finely chopped bottled red peppers
½ cup stale bread crumbs
1 egg yolk
2 teaspoons chopped parsley
¼ teaspoon paprika

Remove stems from mushrooms; reserve for Seasoning. Place mushroom caps in baking dish. Use a plain ⅜-inch pipe to pipe Seasoning into mushroom caps. Bake in moderately hot oven 10 minutes, top with mayonnaise, garnish with pieces of pepper, if desired; serve immediately.

Seasoning: Cook bacon, celery, shallots and garlic in pan until bacon is crisp. Add reserved, finely chopped mushroom stems and peppers, cook further 3 minutes. Place mushroom mixture in bowl, add bread crumbs, egg yolk, parsley and paprika, mix well.

Makes 20.

Front: Shrimp Toasts with Dill Butter; Seasoned Button Mushrooms. Back: Chicken and Asparagus Rolls.

PETITS FOURS

These are well worth the effort, the flavor and texture are delightful. Use your own favorite sponge cake recipe if you like, but we've found the texture of ours to be ideal for easy splitting of the cake; as soon as it's cold it can be split. Prepare cake part up to 2 days before required. Ice and decorate up to a day before serving. Store in cool, dry place—the refrigerator can make the icing sticky.

Sponge Cake (see page 82)
½ cup ground almonds
1 cup apricot jam
2 tablespoons water
1 x 7-oz package almond paste
powdered sugar
12 oz can prepared icing
1 egg white
2 oz semisweet baking chocolate

STEP 1

Make sponge according to recipe on page 82, omitting the cocoa. Beat in the ground almonds. Spread mixture into greased and wax paper–lined 10x6x2-inch baking dish, bake in moderate oven 30 minutes. Turn onto wire rack to cool. Heat apricot jam and water, push jam through sieve to remove any large pieces of fruit. When sponge is cold, split horizontally into four even layers. Line a tin with greaseproof paper, as shown, bringing paper over long sides of tin to make it easy to remove cake from tin. Place top layer of cake, top side down, into lined tin, brush evenly with about a quarter of the jam mixture, continue layering cake and jam until all are used; the last layer of cake should be the base of the sponge.

STEP 2

Brush top of cake with jam. Knead almond paste until smooth with a little sifted powdered sugar, roll to rectangular shape, cut to fit neatly over sponge, place in position over jam, as shown.

STEP 3

Dust top of almond paste lightly with powdered sugar, place another piece of greaseproof paper on top, place another tin over paper (or use thick cardboard cut to shape); weigh down with a brick, or some other heavy object. Refrigerate overnight.

STEP 4

Remove brick, tin and top piece of paper, invert cake onto board. Trim cake to rectangle measuring 10x6-inches, cut into rounds or squares measuring 1¼ inches, stand on wire rack with the almond paste layer on top.

Place icing in top of double saucepan over simmering water, heat gently until icing is warm, stir until smooth, add egg white, stir until smooth. It may be necessary to add a teaspoon or two of water to the icing to bring it to the consistency of pouring cream. Stand cakes (on the wire rack) over a tray to catch the excess icing. Pour or spoon icing over cakes, spread icing around sides as each one is iced. Ice as many cakes as possible, then place excess icing, from tray, back into saucepan, reheat until once again correct consistency, adding more water when necessary. This can be done as often as necessary, providing the icing is not overheated. Leave cakes

to set at room temperature. Decorate with piped melted chocolate, crystallized violets or any small sugar decorations.

Makes about 40 cakes.

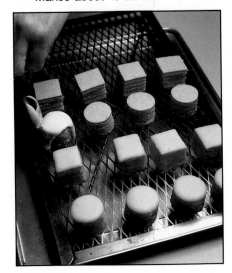

PISTACHIO MINT COLLETTES

If the weather is hot, serve the chocolates in their foil cases. We have given a choice of two Fillings—for variety serve both. Prepare chocolates up to a week before required, store covered in refrigerator.

2 oz pistachio nuts
4 oz dark cooking chocolate
FILLING 1
1½ oz white chocolate
1 tablespoon cream
2 teaspoons butter
½ egg yolk
peppermint oil or essence
green food coloring
FILLING 2
1½ oz dark cooking chocolate
1 tablespoon cream
2 teaspoons butter
½ egg yolk
1 teaspoon rum

Drop pistachios into pan of boiling water, boil for 4 minutes, peel away shell and skin. Chop half finely; grind remaining half finely, reserve for Filling 2.

Melt chopped chocolate over hot water, cool few minutes. Using a teaspoon, spread chocolate inside small foil cases. Refrigerate until set, peel away foil cases if desired. Place Filling into piping bag fitted with fluted tube, pipe into chocolate cases. Sprinkle with pistachio nuts. Store, covered, in refrigerator for up to a week.

Filling 1: Melt chopped chocolate and cream over hot water, cool 5 minutes. Stir in butter and egg yolk, enough peppermint oil or essence to flavor enough green food coloring to color slightly. Beat with wooden spoon until thick.

Filling 2: Melt chopped chocolate and cream over hot water. Remove from heat, cool 5 minutes. Stir in butter and egg yolk, then reserved ground pistachio nuts and rum. Beat with wooden spoon until thick.

Makes about 20.

ALMOND SHORTBREAD DROPS

Store cold cookies in airtight container for up to a week.

3 oz butter
½ cup powdered sugar
1 egg yolk
¾ cup all-purpose flour
⅓ cup ground almonds
red currant jelly
½ cup finely chopped
   blanched almonds

Cream butter, sugar and egg yolk until light and fluffy, stir in sifted flour, then ground almonds. Roll mixture into balls about 1 inch in diameter, place on lightly greased oven trays about 1 inch apart. Press hole in center of each ball with floured finger, spoon in a little red currant jelly, sprinkle lightly with almonds. Bake in moderate oven 15 minutes; cool on trays.

Makes about 30.

SAUSAGE SIZZLE

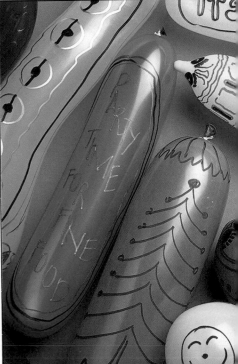

Many cooks who can cope easily with an elaborate dinner party go pale at the thought of catering for a group of kids. Our Sausage Sizzle menu comes to the rescue. It is varied and substantial and has plenty of good, nourishing food included without sacrificing taste and attractiveness.

Quantities are for ten but it depends a bit on the ages and appetites of the children. The menu is best suited to the under-nine-year-olds, but several of the dishes would go over well at teenage parties.

Watch eyes light up as colorful Kim the Caterpillar wriggles her way forward. This great new party cake is easy enough for older children to make for themselves or for younger brothers or sisters.

Remember to have a good backup supply of drinks—cordials, fruit juice and milk. Here are a few suggestions for easy-to-make drinks; also a couple of sauces to serve with sausages for children who prefer something other than ketchup.

CREAMY COLA SPIDER
1.25 liter bottle cola
1 cup vanilla ice cream
1 tablespoon lemon juice
Combine all ingredients, blend in two batches until smooth.
Makes about 10 cups.

ORANGE HONEY WHIP
1½ liters (6 cups) orange juice
3 oranges, peeled, chopped
¼ cup honey
Combine all ingredients, blend in two batches until smooth.
Makes about 10 cups.

CHOCOLATE BANANA SHAKE
1½ liters (6 cups) milk
¼ cup chocolate-flavored topping
3 bananas, chopped
3 eggs
Combine all ingredients, blend in two batches until smooth.
Makes about 10 cups.

TOMATO CHUTNEY SAUCE
¾ cup tomato sauce
¼ cup papaya and mango chutney
2 teaspoons Worcestershire sauce
Combine all ingredients in bowl, mix well.
Makes about 1 cup.

PINEAPPLE SWEET AND SOUR SAUCE
2 x 8-oz cans crushed pineapple
2 teaspoons cornstarch
1 tablespoon honey
1 tablespoon soy sauce
2 teaspoons white vinegar
Blend cornstarch with some of the pineapple syrup, combine with remaining ingredients in pan, stir over heat until sauce boils and thickens.
Makes about 2 cups.

CRUNCHY SAUSAGE ROLLS

Freeze uncooked for up to a month or cook, freeze and reheat when ready to serve.

2 sheets ready rolled puff pastry
1 lb ground steak
2 sticks celery, finely chopped
1 teaspoon Worcestershire sauce
1 tablespoon tomato sauce
2 teaspoons cornstarch
1 egg

Cut each sheet of pastry into 4 even strips both ways to give 16 squares from each sheet.

Combine steak with celery, Worcestershire sauce, tomato sauce and cornstarch, mix well. Take tablespoons of mixture, shape into 2-inch long sausages. Place sausages diagonally across each piece of pastry. Pinch opposite corners together over sausages. Brush pastry with lightly beaten egg; place on lightly greased oven trays, bake in hot oven 20 minutes or until golden brown.

Makes approximately 30.

PITA SAUSAGE ROLLS

Let the children select from the salad vegetables and cheese, wrap the rolls in a napkin or wax paper for easy, no-mess handling.

5 large pita breads
10 thin link sausages
2 carrots, grated
1 small lettuce, shredded
5 oz alfalfa sprouts
2 cups grated cheddar cheese
DRESSING
8-fl-oz bottle Thousand Island dressing
2 tablespoons mayonnaise
1 teaspoon French mustard
2 shallots, chopped

Split each pita bread into two rounds. Barbecue or grill sausages until done. Place a hot sausage on each pita round. Sprinkle with grated carrot, shredded lettuce, sprouts, grated cheese. Spoon on Dressing, roll up pita bread.

Dressing: Combine Thousand Island dressing with mayonnaise, mustard and shallots.

Makes 10.

MARINATED CHICKEN WINGS

Marinate the chicken wings the day before the party.

2¼ lb chicken wings
⅓ cup honey
⅓ cup dry sherry
2 tablespoons soy sauce
1 teaspoon sesame oil
2 tablespoons oil
1 teaspoon ginger
1 clove garlic, crushed
1 teaspoon five-spice powder

Tuck wing tips under each chicken wing. Place in large dish. Combine remaining ingredients in pan, stir over low heat until honey is melted, pour over chicken wings, mix well. Cover and refrigerate few hours or overnight. Grill or barbecue chicken wings, brushing often with marinade until golden brown and tender.

PARTY HOT DOGS

Have the hot dogs rolled in bacon up to a day before the party.

10 long thin frankfurters
2 large dill pickles or gherkins
4 oz cheddar cheese
10 bacon slices
10 frankfurt buns
mustard
tomato sauce
barbecue sauce

Cut almost through frankfurters lengthwise. Cut dill pickles or gherkins into 10 long strips. Place 2 dill pickle strips in 5 frankfurters. Cut cheese into 10 sticks, place 2 sticks of cheese down center of remaining 5 frankfurters. Wrap each frankfurter in a slice of bacon, secure ends with toothpicks.

Grill or barbecue frankfurts until bacon is crisp. Split, toast and butter buns, remove toothpicks from bacon, place in buns. Serve with mustard, tomato or barbecue sauce.

Makes 10.

BARBECUED COCKTAIL FRANKFURTER STICKS

Prepare the day before the party.

2¼ lb cocktail frankfuters
large (about 1½-lb) can pineapple pieces
15-oz can young corn cuts
10 stuffed olives
2 teaspoons French mustard
1 tablespoon brown sugar
1 tablespoon lemon juice

Soak wooden skewers in water several hours or overnight. Cut frankfurters in half. Drain pineapple, reserve syrup, drain corn. Alternate pieces of frankfurt, pineapple, corn and stuffed olives on skewers. Combine reserved pineapple syrup, mustard, brown sugar and lemon juice in pan, bring to boil, boil until reduced to one-third. Brush syrup over both sides of frankfurter sticks, grill or barbecue for a few minutes until hot. Baste with syrup during cooking.

Makes about 20 sticks.

APRICOT COCONUT SLICE

Make and store covered in the refrigerator for up to four days.

8 oz plain sweet cookies
4 oz butter, melted
2 tablespoons apricot jam
8 oz dried apricots, chopped
3½ cups coconut
14½-oz can sweetened condensed milk
½ cup coconut, extra

Crush cookies finely, add melted butter; combine well. Line base of 7x11-inch pan with aluminum foil. Press crumbs evenly over base of tin; refrigerate until firm. Spread base with apricot jam. Place apricots in pan covered with water, bring to boil, remove from heat, cool to room temperature; drain. Combine coconut, condensed milk and apricots, press over cookie base. Place extra coconut on oven tray, bake in moderate oven 8 minutes or until golden brown; cool. Press over apricot mixture. Refrigerate, covered, until firm.

DAISY CAKES

This mixture will make 24 cakes. Cakes will freeze for up to 2 weeks, with or without Vienna Cream and candies.

PATTY CAKES
4 oz butter
1 teaspoon vanilla
⅔ cup sugar
2 eggs
1⅓ cups self-rising four
¼ cup milk
6½-oz package candies
VIENNA CREAM
4 oz butter
1½ cups powdered sugar
2 tablespoons milk

Cream butter, vanilla and sugar, add eggs one at a time, beating well after each addition. Stir in sifted flour and milk alternately, beat until smooth. Place paper patty cases into patty tins. Drop teaspoonfuls of mixture into each patty case. Bake in moderate oven 15 to 20 minutes. Cool on wire rack. When cold, spread top with Vienna Cream, decorate with candies in a daisy pattern.
Vienna Cream: Have butter and milk at room temperature, place butter in small bowl of electric mixer, beat until butter is as white as possible, gradually add about half the sifted powdered sugar, beating constantly, add milk gradually, then gradually beat in the remaining powdered sugar.

CHOCOLATE MINT SLICE

Make and refrigerate up to two days before the party; add the chocolate sprinkles on the day of the party.

8-oz package plain chocolate cookies
4 oz butter melted
2 teaspoons gelatin
½ cup milk
2 x 3-oz packets white marshmallows
peppermint essence
green food coloring
2 x ½-pint cartons cream
chocolate sprinkles

Crush cookies finely, mix in butter. Press evenly over base of 7x11-inch pan, refrigerate. Add gelatin to milk in pan, add marshmallows, stir over low heat without boiling until marshmallows are melted. Remove from heat, add peppermint essence to taste, then stir in a few drops of green coloring; cool to room temperature. Whip cream until thick, fold into marshmallow mixture, pour over chocolate crumb base. Sprinkle with chocolate sprinkles and refrigerate several hours, or cover and refrigerate overnight, then sprinkle chocolate sprinkles on the day of the party.

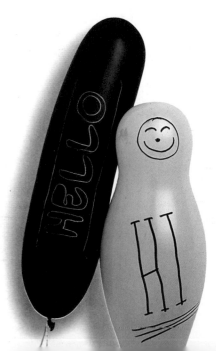

KIM THE CATERPILLAR

We chose to have a striped caterpillar. Divide the Vienna Cream into three bowls, color as desired. We used apricot, purple and green food coloring. Make and decorate the cake up to two days before required. Store in cool, dark, dry place—do not freeze or refrigerate.

1 package butter cake mix
assorted sweets
1 paper-covered board, 12x26 inches
VIENNA CREAM
½ lb butter
3 cups powdered sugar
⅓ cup milk

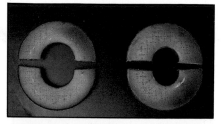

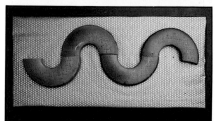

Make cake according to directions on packet. Divide mixture evenly between two greased 8-inch ring pans, bake in moderate oven 30 minutes. Turn onto wire rack to cool. Cut both cakes in half as shown in Step 1. Arrange cakes on covered board as shown in Step 2. Cover top and sides of cakes with colored Vienna Cream. Decorate with assorted sweets.

Vienna Cream: Have butter and milk at room temperature, place butter in small bowl of electric mixer, beat until butter is as white as possible, gradually add about half the sifted powdered sugar, beating constantly, add milk gradually, then gradually beat in the remaining powdered sugar.

DRINKS

Champagne

Champagne is always popular; here are six ways to make it go farther and look prettier. You will need a 750ml bottle to make any one of the recipes to serve four to six people. Make sure the champagne is well chilled, top the glasses slowly to prevent spills; serve immediately.

CHERRY BRANDY COCKTAIL
Place one lump of sugar into each glass. Combine ⅓ cup cherry brandy and ⅓ cup orange juice, divide between glasses, top with chilled champagne.

STRAWBERRY BELLINI
Wash and hull 3 oz strawberries. Puree, process or blend strawberries, add ⅓ cup Grand Marnier, 1 tablespoon sugar (more or less to taste) and 1 teaspoon Grenadine cordial. Divide strawberry mixture between glasses, top with chilled champagne.

CHAMPAGNE BLOSSOM
Combine 1 cup orange juice with ½ cup Cointreau and 1 tablespoon sugar. Stir until sugar is dissolved. Divide mixture between glasses, top with chilled champagne.

GIN AND LEMON BUBBLY
Combine ¼ cup lemon juice with ¾ cup gin and 1 tablespoon sugar. Divide mixture between glasses, top with chilled champagne.

CHAMPAGNE COCKTAIL
Place 1 lump sugar, 1 teaspoon brandy and a good dash of Angostura Bitters into glasses, top with chilled champagne. Decorate with orange segments.

MANGO DELIGHT
Puree pulp of 1 mango, stir in ⅓ cup sugar (more or less to taste) and 1 tablespoon Grand Marnier. Divide mango mixture between glasses, top with chilled champagne.

Frost glasses for your guests by brushing rims of glasses with a little egg white, then dipping in sugar. Pictures below show pretty garnishes for drinks and punches.

Back row: Strawberry, Bellini; Champagne Blossom; Gin and Lemon Bubbly.
Front row: Cherry Brandy Cocktail; Mango Delight; Champagne Cocktail.

Punches

Punches are an inexpensive way of serving a lot of people with a great tasting drink. Make at least two varieties of punches if you're having a party—one with and one without alcohol. The four punches below are so different they could all be made in appropriate quantities for your next party.

WHISKEY CREAM ROYALE
2 liters vanilla ice cream
6 cups hot strong black coffee
2 cups milk
750ml bottle whiskey
1 cup rum
pinch nutmeg

Place ice cream in large bowl, add hot coffee, stir until ice cream is melted. Stir in milk, whisky and rum; cool, chill well. Sprinkle with nutmeg just before serving.
    Makes about 4 liters

How to segment an orange: Peel orange thickly, remove as much white pith as possible. Cut down between each side of each segment close to the membrane that divides each segment.

GINGER, PINEAPPLE AND ORANGE PUNCH
1-liter carton orange juice
750ml can pineapple and orange juice
3 cups water
1 cup sugar
2 x 1.25-liter bottles dry ginger ale
4 oranges, segmented

Combine juices, water and sugar in pan, stir over low heat until sugar is dissolved, cool and chill. Add chilled ginger ale and orange segments just before serving.
    Makes about 5 liters.

LIME TEA PUNCH
3 tea bags
2 cups boiling water
½ cup lime juice
½ cup sugar
½ cup water, extra
1.25-liter bottle lemonade

Pour boiling water over tea bags, stand for 5 minutes, discard tea bags, add strained lime juice; cool. Combine sugar and extra water in pan, stir without boiling until sugar is dissolved, then boil without stirring for 3 minutes. Cool, add to tea mixture, chill. Add chilled lemonade just before serving, decorate with sliced limes and sprigs of mint.
    Makes about 2 liters.

TOMATO VODKA PUNCH
2 x 12-fl-oz cans V-8 vegetable juice
1-liter can tomato juice
⅔ cup lemon juice
1 cup vodka
1 teaspoon Worcestershire sauce
salt, pepper
1 liter soda water

Combine juices, vodka and Worcestershire sauce, season with salt and pepper; chill well. Stir in chilled soda water just before serving. Serve with lemon or lime slices.
    Makes about 3 liters.

Coffee

Make your after-dinner coffee special by topping it with a deliciously flavored whipped cream. There's enough cream to top four large mugs of coffee.

MINT CHOCOLATE COFFEE
Whip ½ cup cream, stir in 1 tablespoon creme de menthe, pipe or spoon onto hot coffee. Top with grated chocolate.

IRISH CREAM COFFEE
Whip ½ cup cream, stir in 1½ tablespoons Irish cream liqueur, pipe or spoon onto hot coffee, sprinkle lightly with cinnamon.

CHOC ORANGE COFFEE
Whip ½ cup cream with ½ teaspoon finely grated orange rind, stir in 1 tablespoon creme de cacao, pipe or spoon onto hot coffee. Decorate with thin slivers of orange rind.

INDEX

OVEN TEMPERATURES:

Electric Temperatures	Farenheit
Very Slow	250°
Slow	300°
Moderately Slow	325–350°
Moderate	375–400°
Moderately Hot	425–450°
Hot	475–500°
Very Hot	525–550°

Gas Temperatures	
Very Slow	250°
Slow	275–300°
Moderately Slow	325°
Moderate	350°
Moderately Hot	375°
Hot	400–450°
Very Hot	475–500°